The Ghost Chasers Motorcycle Club of Spencer, Iowa
by Susan Bendlin Morgan

email: robertsusanmorgan@gmail.com

ISBN: 978-1-62660-181-9

Book and cover design by Michael Campbell, MC Writing Services

THE
Ghost Chasers
Motorcycle Club
OF SPENCER, IOWA

SUSAN BENDLIN MORGAN

For Mom and Dad

CONTENTS

PREFACE

**"Never sell a motorcycle…
it is a part of you."**

ANONYMOUS

The quotation above was a philosophy of my dad, who couldn't bear to sell his Harley Davidson Knucklehead, purchased brand new in 1947, as long as he lived. Indeed, the fact the old bike was a part of him was as clear to us four kids as the fact that we needed to breathe air to stay alive. If we even thought about touching that bike without his permission, not that he would ever grant it, we might not see the light of another day.

Through the years, the old Harley was parked under a tarp in the southwest corner of the Quonset shed on our farm next to the old red and white International Harvester PTO-driven baler. It was a fairly typical shop with all manner of tools and various workbenches and a welder and air compressor where he worked primarily on the maintenance and repair of the farm machinery. Back in the corner was a 7-Up cooler with some bottles of Molson Canadian beer kept ice cold beside a minnow bucket full of bait for a fishing trip, depending on the season. The old farmstead didn't have a garage, and so the Quonset was the nearest protected area for this bike to be stored. If that bike would have fit up the steps and through the front door of the house, he would have parked it in the living room. As he worked on all the worrisome tasks of farming and keeping his family fed, I'm sure it was some comfort to come in from the fields at the end of a long day and be able to glance over and see it there, keeping watch.

The bike didn't sit under the tarp all the time. There were times when dad would get it out and clean it up and start it and get it running just right and take short rides—sometimes in the spring when the snow had melted and the air was the sweetest, sometimes in the summer to ride around the section or over to my grandparents to check if it was time to walk the beans. And he always rode that bike to town in the fall at fair time when he worked at "C Gate" taking tickets. He would park it there in a line of the bikes that all the guys got out to show off at the fair.

When I heard that distinctive deep bass rumble coming from the Quonset and if I hadn't been on his nerves too badly, I would make myself visible and pretend to be studying rocks in the gravel or gazing up at the clouds, giving him a wide berth but also an occasional and hopeful side-eye. If he thought he had the time, he'd give me the nod and say with exasperation, "All right, get over here." I'd run over and he'd point at the bike's exhaust pipes that could reach 500 degrees and give the same stern direction: "Now you keep your leg away from these pipes." And off we would go. And that, to me, was more fun than if I had sprouted wings and could fly.

As a kid, I remember that our farmhouse was a revolving door of his friends and their wives and kids, and I didn't realize at the time that most all of these friendships had been formed through the Ghost Chasers Motorcycle Club. All the young couples met each other, courted, married, and started families through their common interest in riding motorcycles. These friendships were lifelong, with my research often coming across the obituaries of the old members and seeing their pall bearers listed were motorcycle club members.

They had stories, oft repeated, but I was too young to know that the stories were history and history can be easily lost on young ears. It has now been a quarter of a century since his death, and my oldest brother and I just this year decided to look more closely at his treasured keepsakes from those motorcycle riding days. The collection had been placed in a safety deposit box since mom's death over 20 years ago, and we were now ready to decide what should be done with it. Most of these items we began to unwrap I had never handled before, and it had been so ingrained in me to never touch them that I felt guilty—and melancholy—in the task. These feelings were soon overcome by intrigue. We decided to take these items to the Clay County Heritage Center and see what might be done with them.

Upon talking to the director, we found out that the story behind the objects was equally important to the objects themselves. It is one thing to look at a jacket, for instance, and quite another to know who wore it and where and when, etc. And that's how this project began.

The unlocking and documenting of the stories of these young men who banded together and rode as the Ghost Chasers has been a story of mysteries and memories and ghosts. Indeed, I have become a bit of a ghost chaser myself—albeit of another type—struggling to chase down the stories and the details of individuals who lived in another time, decades ago, and most all long dead. In this writing, I hope to do them justice and try to document what happened and with whom.

—*Susan Bendlin Morgan*

1955 Gypsy Tour participants, including Ghost Chasers Motorcycle Club members. Location: Okoboji Speed Bowl

GHOST CHASERS CLUB MEMBERS—PRE-WORLD WAR II

Charter members in 1938–1939

Robert "Bob" Wright, *leader* Bill Stolley

Reyburn "Bob" Fulton, *co-leader* Darrell Ketcham

Bernie Chestelson   Dale Kabrick

Very early members in 1939–1941

Arnold (Bud) Booth   Jesse Young (Sioux Rapids)

Ralph Easton   Al Goyette

Elmer Chestelson (Cornell)

BEGINNING YEARS: 1937-1939

"Four wheels move the body; two wheels move the soul."

ANONYMOUS

The Ghost Chasers Motorcycle Club of Spencer, Iowa, was organized in 1938 by a group of motorcycle-riding friends who became the six charter members of the club. They were Bob Wright, Derril Ketcham, Bernie Chestelson, Dale Kabrick, Bill Stolley, and Bob Fulton. According to newspaper reports, Bob Wright and Bob Fulton were the leaders of that first group and served as club organizers and spokespersons ["Spencer Motorcycle Club Invites," 1939, p. 1]. The group of men who joined the club rode any type of motorcycle—British made, Indian, Harley Davidson, etc. What they had in common was that they all enjoyed the camaraderie of riding their motorcycles with others, and promoting events for motorcycle enthusiasts to enjoy.

The popularity of motorcycles had exploded across the Midwest since 1920, when Harley Davidson—in Milwaukee, Wisconsin—became the largest motorcycle manufacturer in the world, with dealerships in 67 countries and over 28,000 bikes produced. In 1921, Harley Davidson riders went to Daytona and won a half dozen world records in various classes. The record-breaking was topped off by a 110.94-mile-an-hour dash by Leslie "Red" Parkhurst on an 8-valve Harley Davidson.

The company gained even more attention when rider Otto Walker set a speed record on a Harley Davidson the following year. Otto Walker was one of Harley Davidson's first factory riders who set numerous speed records during his eight-year racing career, but the record he set on February 2, 1921, was significant. At a non-title race on a mile board track in Fresno, California, he became the first rider ever to win a motorcycle race at an average speed above 100 m.p.h.

The public was enamored. At the start of the Depression in 1933, sales of new bikes plummeted due to the economy, but the interest of the public in riding motorcycles stayed strong. By the time the Depression ended in 1939, gas was just 19 cents per gallon, and the economical sport of riding motorcycles grew even more.

Motorcycle clubs were starting to organize in many towns across the Midwest by the late 1930s. Clay County, Iowa, provided a near perfect spot for the sport of motorcycle riding, with its abundance of rural roads, scenic green countryside, and nearby lakes. Located at the confluence of the Little Sioux and Ocheyedan Rivers, where Highways 18 and 71 converge, Spencer is the county seat and hub of Clay County. A short jaunt north of Spencer, just 16 miles on Highway 71, one enters the "Iowa Great Lakes" area, where a chain of glacial lakes, including West Okoboji, East Okoboji, Big Spirit Lake, Minnewashta, and Upper and Lower Gar, provide a recreational spot that has been enjoyed for generations. Weekend rides to the lakes for swimming or fishing continues today to be a popular activity for citizens living around Spencer, and one commonly enjoyed by motorcyclists.

The idea for the formation of a Spencer motorcycle club no doubt became quite strong after a local motorcycle gathering at the lakes area in 1937. A *Spencer Daily Reporter* article from May 26, 1937, documents that thirty motorcyclists, belonging to clubs from southern Minnesota and northern Iowa, had participated in a weekend event. The group had spent the night in the lakes area on Saturday, and then enjoyed a Sunday morning ride around the lakes with a stop for Sunday dinner at Red's Place in Arnolds Park.

In the afternoon, the riders moved to the Spirit Lake Airport, located north of Okoboji. There they participated in a motorcycle rodeo and racing. One of the features of the rodeo was a polo game, played atop motorcycles rather than horses, with a mallet used to strike a hard ball and get it through the opposing team's goalpost. Many of the motorcycles held not one, but two passengers which was a common practice of motorcyclists during this time. At the end of the day on Sunday, riders left to go back to their homes.

R.D. Richardson of Forest City, spokesperson for the group and a dealer of Harley Davidsons, along with Victor Graff of Curlew, a dealer of Indian motorcycles, were sponsors of that early meet. In a news article ["Motorcycle Club Holds Outing at Lakes Area Sunday," 1937, p. 5], Richardson explained that the club members meet at a given point, usually every Sunday, to spend the day riding. When riders arrived, a collection was taken up to pay for entertainment and meals.

Riders from area clubs planned to meet in Winnebago, Minnesota, on the following weekend. Richardson stated that the clubs are for the "promotion of friendship among motorcycle owners, and the weekly outings are brief vacations together." It is not known for sure that any of the Spencer Ghost Chasers group, who formed their own club just one year later, were in attendance, but if they weren't they surely took notice of it.

R. D. Richardson and Victor Graff also came to Spencer on Saturday, June 4, 1938, to sponsor a Motorcycle Rodeo at the Clay County Fairgrounds. *The Spencer Daily Reporter* advertisement a few days prior to their visit informed the public that admission to the event was free, though an offering would be taken to cover expenses. The ad says that the rodeo start time is 2:00 p.m. and will include popular motorcycle games of the period: "polo games, wiener biting [sic], digout races [sic], tug-of-war, boot race, egg race, trick riding, balloon bursting, and other stunts all on roaring motorcycles" ["Motorcycle Rodeo," 1938, p. 8]. Many of the creative motorcycle games of the time are still played today at motorcycle rallies.

1930s MOTORCYCLE RODEO GAMES

The wiener biting game is now called the weenie bite game. It is more popular today to call the wiener a hot dog, but both terms refer to the same food item. This game is most often played with a rider and a passenger—usually the passenger is a female. The game starts with competitors riding under a hot dog which has been hung from a string, dangling about six feet from the ground. This string is often attached to a board which is supported perpendicular atop barrels stacked to the side of the course. Each team takes a turn, riding underneath the suspended hot dog. The passenger's job is to stand up from atop the motorcycle and take a large bite out of the hot dog when the motorcycle passes underneath. The winning team is the one that was able to take the largest bite from the hot dog without the rider touching the ground. A variation of the game is with a single rider.

The boot race game requires all riders to remove their boots and place them into one pile behind their lined-up motorcycles. When the starting gun is fired, riders race to the boot pile, find their own pair of boots, get them on, run to their motorcycle, start them up, and race to a finish line. The first one there wins.

The "dig-out" race was typically a short, straight-line sprint of the motorcycles where riders would try to win by being the first to cross the finish. The term "dig-out" referred to the start, when riders would try to be the first off of the starting line, "digging out" of their position. There would likely be no penalties for bumping into other bikes or competitors with safety precautions being minimal.

The egg and spoon race was conducted with the rider of the motorcycle holding a spoon in his mouth with a raw egg balancing in the bowl of the spoon. The rider would need to clamp down on the end of the spoon with his teeth and keep the spoon steady as he rode toward the finish line. The rider to cross the finish line first with the egg intact wins the game.

The "moto-ball" game was played with rules similar to soccer—only atop motorcycles. In the "moto-ball" game, the rider kicked the ball as he rode to the side of it. The objective, just like in soccer, was to get the ball into the opposing team's net.

We can be sure that the Ghost Chasers club members were in attendance, watching (or participating) in the frivolity of the motorcycle rodeo at the Clay County Fairgrounds that day in June, 1938. Their excitement for forming their own club was afire. The six charter members lost no time in organizing their new club, but the next thing they needed to do was find more members.

NEW CLUB SEEKS MEMBERS

On January 26, 1939, a notice in the *Spencer Times* included the headline, "Motorcycle Club to Be Formed Here." This headline in the newspaper makes it sound as if the group is just about to form, but earlier reports (written by members themselves in a 1947 program) saying that the Ghost Chasers had gotten together in 1938 were no doubt accurate.

At first it appears the club was organized informally with a small group of six friends. The newspaper is dated January, 1939, and those original six charter members who had been riding together were now hoping to rally more members for their group and become a fully organized club. This would have required registering the club with the American Motorcycle Association, following some club by-laws, paying dues, and organizing their club's own events in the area. In this article, we find that the club extended an invitation to anyone who owns a motorcycle, or was interested in riding, to attend the meeting in the community room of the Clay County National Bank on Sunday afternoon at 1:30. All wives and girlfriends were graciously invited as well.

This would not be a small meeting. The newly formed Ghost Chasers had also invited members from a Forest City club and received confirmation that twenty to twenty-five were coming to the meeting. To inform the citizens of Spencer about the workings of a motorcycle club and recruit new members, the article says, "There is a national organization of motorcycle clubs. Each club has its own gypsy trips, its hill climbs, races and polo games. Sometimes clubs combine and have trips and meets together." The article goes on to say, "There are ten motorcycle owners in the vicinity of Spencer and other men are reported to be negotiating buying a machine. Tentative plans are being made for a trip through Wisconsin and part of Canada together this summer, and for some good hill climbing meets near Sac City" ["Motorcycle Club to be Formed," 1939, p. 1].

The second meeting to organize the Ghost Chasers Motorcycle Club was held on March 30, 1939, and was again held in the community room of the Clay County National Bank. The Nightcrawlers club from Forest City and motorcyclists from Sac City were invited to this meeting set for Sunday afternoon, and sixty members of those clubs were expected to attend. "All persons interested in cycling are invited to attend" ["Spencer Motorcycle Club Invites," 1939, p. 1].

It is reported that the Ghost Chasers club now numbers eleven Spencer cyclists, headed by Bob Fulton and Bob Wright. The newspaper identified another member by name: Bud Booth. The report says that the Ghost Chasers are very interested in the news that the Sac City club had been quite successful hosting a hill climb the previous year, with 250 machines participating, and they also held a "gypsy hike." In new business, the Ghost Chasers have decided to follow suit and host a local hill climb as early as the coming fall.

The young Ghost Chasers club soon had a regular meeting space in the basement of the Clay County National Bank, and now had "about twelve members," according to an April 13, 1939, article in *the Spencer Times* ["Motorcycle Club Holds Meeting," 1939, p. 7]. Club members have voted to purchase blue silk shirts and plan to sew club emblems on these shirts for their riding regalia. They are also planning to have numerous trips and hill climbs for the coming spring and summer.

Ghost Chasers charter member Bob Wright became a local distributor for Harley Davidson motorcycles by fall. An ad placed in the *Spencer Times* on September 7, 1939, p. 6, states, "New 1940 Harley-Davidson Motorcycles at the Clay County Fair—R.D. Richardson, District Representative... Bob Wright, Local Distributor." Bob Wright had previously registered his own new Harley Davidson on April 5, 1935, according to a notice of new registrations in *The Reporter*.

THE FIRST HILL CLIMB

It takes a great amount of expertise to move a motorcycle up a hill. A very steep hill is usually climbed at just 3 to 4 miles per hour, but balancing on that motorcycle as it bounces and jolts from side to side requires that the driver be adept at balancing and counter steering as he gives the machine the right amount of gas to keep the momentum up. As each successive driver moves to attempt the course, the previous riders have created more and more dips and crevices where their tires come down from airborne jolts with tires spinning and dirt flying. If not careful, he risks falling over backwards.

It is exciting to watch, as there are many spills when the motorcycles get out of control—and it is also possible to go airborne and flip over if there is too much momentum. This can easily occur if the driver is heavy on the throttle with the front tire in the air when the rear tire engages with the dirt. Often the bikes are wisely abandoned in a sideways lurch and must be "caught" by designated helpers or excited onlookers—often being adrenalin-filled teenage boys. The bikes must be stopped from their plunge to the bottom of the hill before the bikes are destroyed or they injure spectators.

In addition to expertise, the driver must be fit. This is a competition which will put tremendous strain on the driver's abdomen, glutes, upper thighs, and lower back muscles. The motorcycles used in 1937 had an average weight of 565 pounds, and in a hill climbing situation, the driver must be strong enough to manhandle the machine while gripping the handlebars and working to maneuver it as it jolts in every direction but straight.

The spot on the hill where the motorcycle with its driver ends their forward motion is marked and measured in number of feet. If the motorcycle with its driver makes it over the top, then the contest is measured in number of seconds it took for the rider to get over the top.

The Ghost Chasers motorcycle club was off to a rocky start in the organization of their first hill climb, as evidenced by a highlighted article in the *Spencer Times* dated September 20, 1939. It was also possible they had not yet settled on a club name. The headline reads, "Wanted at Once! A HILL—!" The newspaper says, "The Spencer Motorcycle Club, better known as the 'Ghost Riders', are at present hunting this area over, high and low, for a hill, the hill however can be only high—and steep. The reason for this great search is that some half-dozen clubs have been invited to Spencer for a week from Sunday to participate in hill climbing events, and it wasn't until after the invitations were in the mail and on their way to their destinations that someone remembered the minor detail of finding a suitable hill had not been checked into. However, the members of the club are apparently unworried as they are quite certain the missing hill will turn up in time" ["Wanted at Once," 1939, p. 5].

It is no surprise that the club was unconcerned about the exact location of this first hill climb, as hills were a dime a dozen throughout Clay County, Iowa. The topography of the Little Sioux River is such that hills of all shapes and sizes are typical along its meandering banks. The tilled ground of the farms looped around these hilled banks, and it was not uncommon for areas along the river to be left to the wildlife. The club just needed to secure permission from the nearby farmer to be allowed to use the area and make sure that attendees and their parked cars did not disturb crop ground.

The group invited clubs from Forrest City, Ames, Sioux City, and Estherville to attend the hill climb. The motorcycle membership list is reported to have included Bob Wright, Dale Kabrick, Bill Stolley, Darrel Ketcham, Bud Booth, Bob Fulton, and Bernie Chestelson.

Further research showed that the club did indeed find a hill. But rather than hold the hill climb on October 1, as the previous article reported, it was not held until Sunday, October 8. This may have been because of the issue with finding a location for the hill climb, or it may have been because the nearby town of Estherville was planning a hill climb of their own on October 1.

Another *Spencer Times* news story, this one dated Thursday, October 5, 1939, tells us, "Spencer Motorcycle Club Hill Climb Sunday." The newspaper uses Ghost Chasers as the club's name at the beginning of the article, but ends the article calling the club the Ghost Riders. It says, "The Spencer Motorcycle Club, who have dubbed themselves the Ghost Chasers, will stage an afternoon of thrilling entertainment next Sunday afternoon when they will play hosts to numerous representatives of other motorcycle clubs in northwest Iowa at a hill climb two miles east of Spencer on Highway 18" ["Spencer Motorcycle Club" 1939, p. 5].

The club's October 1939 event was the very first hill climb organized by the Ghost Chasers, and the very first hill climb ever held in Spencer. The article states, "Three separate motorcycle climbing events will be held, as well as a bicycle climb, which will precede the motor events." The report said that all-stock machines would be used for the climbs, including an event for motorcycles equipped without chains as well as those equipped with chains. "Clubs from Sioux City, Forest City, Estherville, and Ames have been sent invitations by the Spencer club and have signified their intention to participate in the events. The hill climb will begin promptly at 2 p.m."

According to the article, the "Ghost Riders" included, among others, Bob Wright, Dale Kabrick, Bill Stolley, Darrel Ketcham, Bud Booth, Bob Fulton, and Bernie Chestelson. These are the same seven members mentioned in the article ["In an Out," 1939, p. 3] but there are five other members yet to be identified: total membership is reported as being "eleven members" ["Motorcycle Club Invites," 1939, p. 1].

A second quarter-page advertisement was placed in the *Spencer Times* on Thursday, October 5, 1939, to catch the attention of the newspaper's readers. From this advertisement we find that the admission to the hill climb was 25 cents, with children under ten admitted free, and prizes to be awarded to winners. They advised spectators that "if you wish to spend an afternoon enjoying the sights of thrills and spills, be sure and see this entertainment." The location is disclosed. The hill climb was to be held 2 miles east of Spencer on U.S. Highway 18. The club's planning included a rain date of October 15th.

The weekend before the planned Spencer hill climb, a few members of the Ghost Chasers traveled to Estherville to witness and take part in that town's hill climb. [In and Out of Spencer, 1939, p. 3.] Attendees were Mr. and Mrs. Robert Wright, Bernie Chestelson, Bob Fulton, and Bud Booth. Bill Stolley and Dale Kabrick from Spencer also attended. Since the Ghost Chasers first hill climb was planned for the following weekend and they had invited many clubs, these young men must have been watching closely with many questions as to how their own hill climb should be run.

The *Spencer Times* article on Thursday, October 5, 1939, exclaims, "Spencer Motorcycle Club Hill Climb Sunday." It was three days before the Ghost Chasers are going to stage the town's first ever hill climb. The paper reports that clubs from Sioux City, Forest City, Estherville, and Ames have signified their intention to attend. The promoters of the hill climb promise "thrilling entertainment" for spectators.

This first ever hill climb was a success, according to the *Spencer Times* report printed on October 12 ["350 See Motorcycle Hill Climbing Events," 1939, p. 5]. Twenty-one riders entered the various events, while 350 citizens came out to observe the action. Riders from Sioux Falls, Sioux City, Fort Dodge, Forrest City, Estherville, Badger, Swea City, Buffalo Center, and Spencer attended. Local rider Darrel Ketcham entered the hill climb events representing the Ghost Chasers. This must have been quite a hill, as only one rider was able to make it clear to the top of the incline that afternoon: a rider from Swea City, Walt Orens, who did so in 18 seconds. The total length he went with his first-place finish is not listed, but other racers who did not get to the top placed with measurements from 51 feet to 90 feet. The club included a bicycle hill-climbing event just prior to the motorcycle runs, won by a Spencer youth, George Sayre.

The hill climb activities and the fun rides these members of the Ghost Chasers were enjoying must have served as a great respite from the world's growing trouble. Many of these young men would be basking in their last months of carefree fun and freedom. World War II was looming, Germany had invaded Poland on September 1, 1939, and the sobering winds of war were upon the entire country. All Ghost Chasers club members would soon be registering for the draft. Many would disperse into military service, and the country would be shut down with rationing of gasoline and necessities. But before this happened, and possibly in defiance of it, Ghost Chasers club members would make the most of the time they had and hold two more hill climbs in the next two years.

1940: THE SECOND HILL CLIMB AT THE GUY HUGINON FARM

June 6, 1940, a *Spencer Times* article reported ["In and Out of Spencer," p. 3] that several Spencer Ghost Chasers members attended a hill climb in Sioux Falls on Memorial Day. The listed members are Mr. and Mrs. Ralph Easton, Mr. and Mrs. Robert Wright, and Bud Booth.

A half page ad in the *Spencer Times* on June 27, 1940, informed the citizens of Spencer that there would be a hill climb sponsored by the Ghost Chasers Motorcycle Club on Sunday, July 14. It would take place 2½ miles east of Spencer on Highway 18, which is the same location as the first hill climb last year. The ad said there would be four events for stock machines. The first event would be "45 cubic inch." The second would be "74-61-80 cu. Inch," the third would be "45 cubic inch with chains," and the fourth event would be "74-61-80 cu. inch with chains." Preceding the event was a bicycle climb. In 1940, Harley Davidson motorcycles were often referred to by their engine displacement, measured in cubic inches. This practice helped to distinguish between different models and their performance capabilities.

The *Spencer Times* printed an article on July 4, 1940, titled, "Many Entries Listed… Motorcycle Hill Climb Is Set for Next Sunday." They reconfirm that this is the second annual hill climb for the Ghost Chasers, to be held July 14. Many entries were expected, and numerous motorcycle clubs were expected to attend the hill climb "in force." ["Motorcycle Hill Climb," 1940, p. 5] said, "The site of the climb, which is located on the Guy Huginon farm on Hwy. 18 offers spectators full view of the entire proceedings from a shaded area, and a large crowd is expected to witness the event. Master of ceremonies of the event will be Ralph Easton, who together with Bob Wright and Reyborn (Bob) Fulton have been in charge of arrangements for the contest."

The citizens of Spencer were surely convinced they would have an exciting time, as the sports writing from this era is especially colorful. ["Motorcycle

Hill Climb," 1940, p. 5] "Last year's winner, Walt Owens of Swea City, the only one to go over the top, will be back again to defend his championship. However, he will have keen competition from some of the finest and most daring motorcyclists in five states. Among these will be Bill Felton of Sioux City, who is renowned throughout the Middlewest, and Anc Hahn of Kansas City, who is considered tops in motorcycle daring. Ray Moore of Ames, a rough and tumble rider who specializes in thrills; Harry Dilges of Ft. Dodge, one of the high scorers in last year's climb; Bob Sanders and Joe Seek, both of Sioux City, who have a private feud of their own; Bobby Barlsow of Swea City, who rolled his entire machine down the complete length of the hill last year after reaching the top; and Gus Johnson of Badger, Iowa, will be among the many others who have signified that they will compete.

"The Ghost Chasers will be represented in the competition by Darrel Ketcham, who has made a name of his own in this area as a daring rider. He will use a new machine in the contest."

The *Spencer Daily Reporter* printed an article on July 10, 1940, titled, "Cycle Event Set July 14." The article informs us that the Ghost Chasers club has been active for two years, and had their first hill climb the year before. They explain that the regular activities of the club include excursions through the area by a large group almost every Sunday. And on the next day, July 11, 1940, there is a follow-up article in *The Spencer Daily Reporter*, "Cycle Daredevils Will Compete Near Spencer."

The hill that the motorcycle riders will attempt to climb is described as "a steep bluff hill" and one or two local machines will be "on the starting line ready for the gun in this dangerous competition." The article explains more about the motorcycles ["Cycle Daredevils," 1940, p. 1]. "Four big events are open to machines of 45 cubic inch… and another group will participate in the 61-74-80. The first event will be the climb without chains for the 45-inch machines. This will be followed by a climb for the same cycles outfitted with chains." The local leader of the Ghost Chasers is identified as Bob Wright.

A second half-page ad appeared in the *Spencer Times* July 11, 1940, reminding the public that the hill climb was coming up on Sunday, July 14. This ad was identical in content to the ad run on June 27th.

Spencer had a population of around 6,500 citizens at this time. The news they received came either from radio, newspapers, or word of mouth. In rural Clay County, the REA was working hard to establish electrical service to farm homes, but only about half of the rural homes had been reached. Rural telephones were all on multi-family party lines, and not every house had one. Television had been invented, but only 8000 families in the entire United States owned a TV and very few, if any, were in the town of Spencer. It is impressive that these six young men could start up a motorcycle club and convince such a large crowd of townspeople to gather on that bluff 2½ miles from town on Guy Huginon's farm to watch this hill climb on that Sunday afternoon in the summer of 1940. But that is exactly what they did. The day after the hill climb, on July 16, 1940, page one of the *Spencer Daily Reporter* says, "1000 Watch Cycles Race Up Hillside."

"200 motorcycles lined the highway and 38 machines were seen in active competition. The snorting two-wheeled racers came from a radius of 200 miles in every direction. The events got underway at 2:00 p.m. with cars parked in every available space, and bright-colored clothing splashed through the crowd, and the roaring machines adding color to the event. No injuries were reported in the course of the thrilling events, but one machine jolted the driver off and crashed through a fence, and another rider lost control of his mount on the hillside and rolled over and down the hill" ["1000 Watch," 1940, p. 1]. Club members told the reporter that a cross-country dash is on their upcoming calendar of events.

Not to be outdone, the *Spencer Times* echoed the report of 1000 people attending. The Thursday after the climb, on July 18, 1940, they ran a similar headline. "Sioux City Wins Meet… 1000 Attend Hill Climb Sunday." This article reports ["1000 Attend Hill Climb," 1940, p. 5.], "Thrills galore were given the crowd by the 38 contestants. One machine, ridden by Coderman, turned over backwards and catapulted down the hill after climbing some

80-odd feet. Coderman was thrown clear of the machine, thus escaping injury. Around 250 motorcycles were crowded into the woods at the site of the meet, with the most colorful events being the machines with chains."

The motorcycles threw dirt in every direction as they climbed the hill, scattering the spectators in nearly every attempt who crowded closely all around. A photo accompanying the article shows people—women, teenagers, and men—crowded within just a few feet of the course to see the next rider make the rise. There were no barricades, no "keep back" rules, and spectators would have been able to reach out and touch the riders as they tried to stay on top of their struggling mounts and get through the tape at the top.

One winner, Bill Felton of Sioux City, got over the top of the hill and "treated" the crowd to a record-breaking time of 4.8 seconds in the 45 cubic-inch with chains event.

The final large event of 1940 was attended by over 300 area motorcyclists, held at the Buena Vista County Fairgrounds in neighboring Alta, Iowa, on Sunday afternoon, September 29, rather than the hometown fairgrounds in Spencer. It seems there was a bit of a misunderstanding that occurred regarding this competition, which was to include a variety of motorcycle activities on a fairgrounds track. First, the event was announced to be happening at Clay County Fair, and next it was announced the event had moved to the Buena Vista County Fairgrounds due to "lack of cooperation on the part of some of the officials." ["Schedule Motorcycle Races at Alta Sunday," 1940, p. 5.] According to Bob Fulton, spokesman for the motorcycle club, he advised the public to come early to assure they got good seats, as "several thousands" were expected to attend. He said that the events would include fasttrack races, tough track races, motorcycle polo, stunt riding, and novelty contests, with over 300 motorcyclists participating. According to Fulton, a large number of Spencer and Clay County riders would be among the participants.

The excitement of these motorcycle events must have been a great respite from the worry looming over the country. In world news, Germany had invaded Norway and Denmark in April that spring. This was followed by an offensive into the Netherlands, Belgium, and France, ultimately leading to the fall of France in June. German air raids on Britain began, known as "The Blitz." The Auschwitz concentration camp began operation in May. By October, all men in the United States between the ages of 21 and 35 were required to register for the draft. The United States was gearing up for war. All of these young Northwest Iowa riders were within this age range, and were obviously very fit for duty.

DRAFT REGISTRATION CARDS FOR GHOST CHASERS CLUB MEMBERS

Bob Fulton: Robert Reyborn Fulton registered for the draft on 16 October, 1940, age 24 (D.O.B. 25 January, 1916). Height 5'9"; Weight 170; Eye color: Brown; Hair color: Black; Complexion: Dark.

Bob Wright: Robert L. Wright registered for the draft on 16 October, 1940, age 34 (D.O.B. 5 December, 1906). Height 5'7"; Weight 155: Eye color: Brown; Hair color: Brown; Complexion: Dark. Employed at H & N Chevrolet; Enlisted in Navy, served from 26 May, 1942–21 October, 1945.

Arnold "Bud" Booth: Arnold William Booth registered for the draft 1 July, 1941, age 21 (D.O.B. 30 May 1920). Height 5'9"; Weight 145; Eye color: Hazel; Hair color: Brown; Complexion: Light. Served in the military from 2 October, 1941-2 December, 1945.

Darrel Ketcham: registered for the draft 16 October, 1940, age 21 (D.O.B. 26 February, 1919). Height: 6'4"; Weight: 200; Eye color: Blue; Hair color: Brown; Complexion: Ruddy. Profession: self employed.

Bernie Chestelson: Bernie Lauris Chestelson registered for the draft 16 October, 1940, age 34 (D.O.B. 23 May, 1906). No height or weight written on card, Eye color: Blue; Hair color: Blonde; Complexion: Light; Profession: carpenter. Served in the Navy from July 15, 1941-January 1, 1949, stationed at Air Station Argentia, Newfoundland.

Dale Kabrick: Dale Eugene Kabrick registered for the draft 16 October, 1940, age 23 (D.O.B. 1 July, 1917). Height 5'11"; Weight 170; Eye color: Blue; Hair color: Brown; Complexion: Light; Profession: farmer.

Bill Stolley: William Nelson Stolley registered for the draft 16 October, 1940, age 25 (D.O.B. 25 July, 1915). Height: 6' 1"; Weight: 205; Eye color: Blue; Hair color: Brown; Complexion: Light; Profession: farmer.

Jess Young: Jesse Monroe Young registered for the draft 16 October, 1940, age 24 (D.O.B. 30 Dec. 1915). Height: 5' 10"; Weight 175; Eye color: Gray; Hair Color: Brown; Complexion: Dark; Profession: mechanic.

Ralph Easton: Ralph Wilbur Easton registered for the draft 16 October, 1940, age 27 (D.O.B. 8 Jan 1913). Height: 5' 11"; Weight 175; Eye color: Blue; Hair color: Brown; Complexion: Light; Birth mark on left temple; profession: self-employed at Jones Music House.

Al Goyette: Albert Lloyd Goyette registered for the draft 16 October, 1940, age 24 (D.O.B. 10 Aug. 1916). Height: 5' 3"; Weight 143; Eye color: Blue; Hair color: Black; Complexion: Dark; Profession: Asher Motors; Served in the military during WWII.

GHOST CHASERS CLUB MEMBER
RALPH EASTON: "THE CROONER"

All of the early Ghost Chasers members have their own stories to be told, but there is one member who was truly an interesting character. When I interviewed Ghost Chaser member Paul Currans in 2024, he told me there was an early Ghost Chaser member, Ralph Easton, who was famous for playing in a trio at the lakes. Newspaper articles from late 1930s tell a story of Ralph Easton as a young man often playing music with two or three friends, and also singing at social gatherings and weddings.

Within a few years he became the featured vocalist for "Jack Reams and his Orchestra," traveling to ballrooms across the Midwest. He was described as a "crooner." The band described themselves as having a "boogie-woogie" style. Famous crooners of that time were Bing Crosby, Perry Como, and Frank Sinatra. The songs that they, and Ralph Easton, sang were songs such as "Sentimental Journey," "'Til the End of Time," and the number one Christmas song of that time period: "White Christmas."

The Jack Reams Orchestra not only played locally—at the Tangney Hotel for a Holiday Ball Junior Chamber event, at the Woodcliff ballroom near Spencer, and at the Central Ballroom at Arnolds Park, but they also toured, playing at the Washington Hotel in Indianapolis, Indiana, and other cities across the upper Midwest.

At one point the band had an extended engagement in Kansas City, Missouri, and Ralph Easton—along with his growing family—rented their home in Spencer to move there for a period of time. In addition, Ralph Easton had his own band, advertised locally as "Ralph Easton and his Orchestra," and also as the "Ralph Easton Trio." In 1947, Ralph Easton played at the Oak Logvillion in Sioux Rapids on Saturday, July 12, at a dance sponsored by the Sioux Rapids American Legion and Lions Club. There can be found a multitude of events in area newspaper advertisements of the time where Ralph Easton was the headliner playing at a dance. He played at the Orleans at the lakes, the Sioux Valley Log Cabin, and the Central Ballroom in Arnolds Park nearly every weekend from 1947–1974.

Ralph Easton seems an unlikely character to belong to a motorcycle club. It is not found that he entered any hill climbs or races on his bike. During the summer of 1940 he and his wife attended motorcycle hill climbs and races in Algona and in Sioux Falls with Mr. and Mrs. Bob Wright and other members of the Ghost Chasers. He was the master of ceremonies for the Ghost Chasers at one of the early hill climbs, in addition to helping organize it, according to newspaper reports.

When he got married, he was working at the Spencer Gambles store. He was transferred to the town of Cherokee to work in the Gambles store there shortly after his marriage. He and his wife lived in Cherokee for two years, and then he was given a promotion to assistant manager at a Gambles store opening in Idaho Falls, Idaho. There he spent three years before returning to Spencer, where he worked repairing band instruments at Jones Music House.

In the years that followed, he became a member of the Spencer Junior Chamber of Commerce, served on their board of directors, and in his spare time he continued to play music and entertain. It is not known how many years he was a member of the Ghost Chasers, but it appears that, like so many other members, a growing family and responsibilities took him away from that frivolity.

1941: THRILL DAY EXPOSITION, GROUP FUN RIDES, AND TT RACES AT THE NEW MOTORCYCLE SPORTING COURSE

The Ghost Chasers first gathering of 1941 was a dinner party held in the community rooms of the Clay County Bank on January 26. Over 70 people attended, including members and guests from many area towns. Dinner was served at 1:30, and afterwards they spent the afternoon dancing and playing cards ["Ghost Chasers Are Hosts," January 30, p. 4].

From an article in the *Spencer Daily Reporter* on April 18 ["Thrill Day," 1941, p. 6], it is found that the Ghost Chasers held an election of officers. Bob Wright was elected for his second term as president, Bud Booth elected as secretary, and Darrell Ketcham elected the road captain. Jess Young as club referee would officiate at all events of the Ghost Chasers.

It was common for clubs to elect a president, a vice-president, and a secretary-treasurer. What is unique to motorcycle clubs is the need for an elected road captain. The members of the Ghost Chasers were taking weekend rides in every direction as part of their club activities. The road captain had some very specific duties in relation to these rides. He was the one responsible for planning the route and making sure there were no hazards along the route for riders. Often the road captain would pre-ride the route to identify any issues. His job was to keep an eye on the weather conditions and communicate any changes to the group. It would be the road captain who would also brief the group before the ride, making sure the group was aware of the plan, and advise the riders about planned gas stops, restaurant stops, or other points of interest, often acting as a tour guide. In addition, the road captain would lead the group, accept the responsibility for ensuring safety of the riders, and check to make sure everyone arrived at the destination.

Another office held in the club was that of club referee, a "referee in chief" or RIC. The person holding this office was considered one of the most important members of the AMA racing ecosystem. It was the club referee's job to ensure fair play by enforcing the rules during sanctioned competitions. Sioux Rapids resident Jess Young was a great choice for this office as he had personal experience competing in AMA races and hill climbs, and was well aware of the rule book. He was also very popular with the general motorcycle riding public and respected by other racers.

This April newspaper article also reports that the Ghost Chasers have been invited to stage a "Thrill Day" in August at the Buena Vista Fair in Alta. This is the first evidence of trick riding, or thrill riding, reported for members of the Ghost Chasers. They had leased the Buena Vista Fairgrounds track the previous summer of 1940 for their own enjoyment, and a large number of spectators had expressed interest in seeing them at the fair, which explains their invitation ["Thrill Day," 1941, p. 6].

The town of Alta is just about an hour's drive southwest from Spencer, traveling on Highway 71 and passing through the town of Sioux Rapids. The fairgrounds in Alta is friendly toward motor sports even to this day. Their grandstand events bring in large crowds of fans to watch summer tractor pulls, motocross races, and stock car races.

The Ghost Chasers made the news again in the month of April. Their club's first official "turn-out" of the year was planned for April 27. The *Spencer Times* reported that 20 or more riders were expected to participate in a club ride and picnic ["Ghost Chasers Start Season's Activities," 1941, p. 5]. After the event was held, the *Spencer Daily Reporter* confirmed that 25 machines had been buzzing all over the countryside as the Ghost Chasers held their annual spring picnic ["Ghost Chasers Hold Picnic," 1941, p. 6]. It is probable that the club included some fun competition in this turn-out day, and had given the impression of buzzing around various sites on the rural roads.

A flurry of activity continued for the members of the Ghost Chasers as they promoted a new event. An advertisement published in the *Spencer Daily Reporter* on June 6, 1941, informed the public that the Ghost Chasers would be hosting motorcycle races on June 8th. They planned three feature events with riders from four states having entered ["Motorcycle Races Sunday," 1941, p. 6.]. The very interesting thing about these races is that they were held at the same location as the previous hill climbs—2½ miles east of Spencer on Highway 18.

Coverage of the races appeared in the *Spencer Daily Reporter* on June 9, 1941. The races held at the now-named Motorcycle Sporting Course were TT Races. The term TT Race originated in 1907 with a Tourist Trophy race held on the Isle of Man in the U.K. The races were originally intended for touring machines, which were street-legal motorcycles. The term "TT Race" became commonly used to describe any dirt track motorcycle race which contained both right and left hand turns, and a few steeplechase-style jumps.

The races sponsored by the Ghost Chasers were well attended that day in June despite cold damp weather. The newspaper described the course, saying that it was "not on the typical straight or oval track. Rather, the course ran over rough terrain in a twisting route which called for gear shifts at numerous points and highly skillful handling.

"Ole Cordornan of Ringsted was the winner in the 80 cubic inch race while a Ghost Chaser pilot, Darrell Ketcham of near Spencer, came in second in that event. Ketcham brought more honor to the local riders by placing second in the open event. Ketcham, the burly road captain for the Ghost Chasers, handled his machine beautifully Sunday and brought cheers from the crowd and praise from his fellow riders for his riding.

"Only one mishap of anywhere near a serious nature marred the events here Sunday. In one of the events, two machines, snorting side by side, became locked together, whirled off the course, and into a tree. One of the riders was taken to Spencer for medical treatment, but he was reported only slightly injured" ["Many Watch Cycle Club Event," 1941, p. 1].

1941: HILL CLIMB #3

The Ghost Chasers went on to sponsor their third annual hill climb during the summer of 1941. The *Spencer Times* informed the public "over forty entries from four states will give the Ghost Chasers a record-breaking field for their upcoming hill climb set for this Sunday, July 20." This article reported that the Ghost Chasers club members who were expected to enter this climb included Ralph Easton, Darrell Ketcham, Jesse Young, Al Goyette, Bob Fulton, Bud Booth, and Bob Wright, who they say "will probably line up" ["Large Number Entries," 1941, p. 5]. The spokesperson for the club says that the proceeds for this race are going to be used to build the Ghost Chasers a club house.

The *Spencer Daily Reporter* echoed the *Spencer Times* that same day, July 17, saying that over 200 machines were expected to gather for the hill climb. "Hill climb contestants are scheduled to come from four states to send their bucking iron horses hurtling up the hillside" ["Hill Climb Sunday," 1941, p. 5].

The club paid for a large advertisement in The *Spencer Daily Reporter* published on July 18, advising the public of the hill climb coming up on Sunday, sponsored by the Ghost Chasers. The ad says it is the club's "annual" hill climb and will be held at the riding grounds 2½ miles east of Spencer on Highway 18. This is the same location as the first hill climb—at Guy Huginon's property. Admission will be 25 cents for everyone over twelve.

The Spencer Daily Reporter tells us what happened at the hill climb the previous Sunday: "Record is Shattered in Hill Climb Meet." Readers learn that Bill Felton from Sioux City has shattered the 45 smooth tire event at the Sunday hill climb by topping the hill in a time of 3 seconds flat. The second-place time in that event was 4.4 seconds. Ghost Chasers member Darrell Ketcham took second in the 80 smooth tire event with a time of 4 seconds. "As the burly Ketcham topped the rise with his machine, just broke the tape in fact, his machine looped completely over giving a weird display of flying wheels and legs. Ketcham was uninjured however" ["Record Shattered," 1941, p. 6].

The Spencer Times reported on the hill climb as well: "New Hill Climb Record Set at Motor Cycle Event," July 24, 1941, p. 8. A full list of all events and rider's placings along with their hill climb times was listed in the article. A detail provided about the record setting hill climb run by Bill Felton included that he was riding an Indian motorcycle. The report says that he broke his previous record by more than one second.

BUENA VISTA FAIR THRILL DAY PERFORMANCE, A PARADE, AND A WEDDING

The *Sioux Rapids Press* published an ad on July 31, 1941, for the upcoming 55th Annual Buena Vista County Fair to be held in Alta, Iowa, on August 12–15. The day-by-day fair schedule includes the information that Friday would be a "Thrill Day with Northwest Iowa's 'Ghost Chasers' Motorcycle Club" ["55th Annual Buena Vista Fair," 1941, p. 3]. An hourly schedule was also printed in the *Sioux Rapids Press,* with an article "Fine Program Arranged for County Fair." The time set for the Ghost Chasers performance was 2:00 p.m. on Friday.

On August 7, 1941, another article was printed in the *Sioux Rapids Press.* "County Fair Next Week" is the headline and again the public was reminded that Friday, August 14, is Thrill Day with "Northwest Iowa's Ghost Chasers, widely known motorcycle daredevils, doing spine-tingling stunts."

There is no eyewitness or newspaper account of any spine-tingling stunts performed by the Ghost Chasers on that August afternoon, although it was reported that the audience did cheer at their racing abilities. One would expect to see a few of the various stunts performed in thrill day expositions across the country at that time, and certainly a repeat of the stunt riding and motorcycle polo that the Ghost Chasers had performed right there in Alta the year before.

There could have been shenanigans such as riding while standing atop a speeding bike with no hands on the handlebars—often done in a line of bikes with all riders performing the same trick. Quite possibly there would have been a display of multiple passengers balancing on one moving bike, often performed with as many as four people; the driver would hold a man atop his shoulders, another rider would face backwards and ride on the front fender, and another rider would climb on the rear of the bike and balance in various aerial positions.

Many of the traveling motorcycle troupes appearing at county fairs at the time performed with a motorcycle zooming up a ramp, launching in the air, and coming down on another ramp a distance away. In between the two ramps would often be individuals lying on the ground with the threat of annihilation looming overhead. It was typical for the finale of a motorcycle thrill show to be a ring of fire with a motorcyclist riding through the flames, or a wall of fire for the motorcycle to crash through.

The newspaper account in the *Spencer Daily Reporter* on August 16, 1941, does not report any antics such as these, although a few of them may have occurred. The report says that hundreds of spectators cheered the daring riders in the Thrill Day Events in Alta, Iowa. "The highlight of the day was Bill Felton's half-mile jaunt around the dirt track in 28 seconds flat" ["Ghost Chasers Sponsor Thrill Day," 1941, p. 6].

Bill Felton was from Sioux City and a frequent and popular winner of the area motorcycle races. The final championship open race that day was ten laps around the track, won by Whit Hemingway, with Bill Felton in second, after they had "staged a stirring duel up and down the track." Can you imagine the smell of roasted peanuts, popcorn, cotton candy, hot August heat, and the carnival sounds in the background drowned out by the smell of exhaust and the roar of the Ghost Chasers motorcycles spinning up dust clouds around the fair race track? It must have been a fabulous show for one and all.

What was next for the Ghost Chasers? They ended their year of events by leading the way at the front of a parade held in Spencer on October 19, 1941. This five-block-long parade was part of the festivities held by Eagles lodge members from all of Northwest Iowa who had gathered in Spencer for their district meeting. Over 700 Eagles members and their families had come to town. The town of Spencer turned out to welcome them. The parade included first the Ghost Chasers on their motorcycles, then the marching bands, floats, and several autos, and the Spencer High School band brought up the rear ["Eagles Hold District Meeting," 1941, p. 1].

Ghost Chasers Motorcycle Club leading parade circa 1940s
(Photo courtesy of the Singelstad family, G. White)

The Ghost Chasers did make some additional headlines before the year was over. The hometown hill climber, Darrell Ketcham, married Velma Borst. It was a lovely wedding held on Sunday afternoon, November 2. The reason attention was widespread was due to the send-off. In true Ghost Chasers fashion, "instead of a car, Darrell had his motorcycle. And it was decorated with all the usual streamers and tin cans and so forth that the witty usually tie on the autos of the newlyweds. About umpteen of the members of the 'Ghost Riders' took off after them on their two wheeled thunderbolts also. Looked like the advance guard of the mechanized cavalry deploying into action" [Beck, 1941, p. 9].

Then on December 7, 1941, the Japanese attacked Pearl Harbor. 2,403 Americans died. The next day Franklin D. Roosevelt delivered his famous "Day of Infamy" speech before a joint session of Congress and a nationwide radio audience. We can be certain that the citizens in and around Spencer had their chairs pulled up close to the radio as war was declared on Japan, and the United States was finished with its isolationism. Roosevelt's speech was a call to arms for the entire population. There would be a sudden shift to a war footing that meant wage and price controls, immediate rationing of food, fuel, and other strategic materials, and of course, induction into the service of husbands, sons, fathers, and sweethearts.

No doubt the Ghost Chasers club had a more somber event than the one they had originally planned as a festive end to their season. They advertised in the *Spencer Daily Reporter* on December 10—just a few days after the attack on Pearl Harbor—that they were hosting a carnival dance on December 11 at the Woodcliff in Spencer ["Annual Carnival Dance," 1941, p. 5]. The Woodcliff Ballroom was within throwing distance of Guy Huginon's farm, where the previous summer had seen large crowds at the hill climb and races. This carnival dance had just been turned into a going away party for many in the crowd as the storm of war erupted.

1942: WORLD WAR II QUIETS THE CLUB— EXCEPT FOR A FREEDOM PARADE

The Ghost Chasers Motorcycle Club shut down plans for any hill climbs or races or "thrill days" in 1942. The country was at war. Rationing of essential goods became necessary to support the troops with supplies, and take care of supply and demand issues across the country. The first rationed item, starting in January, was tires. Consumers could no longer purchase new tires. Tires were allowed to be patched or the treads replaced. Gasoline was rationed starting in May, and by summertime even bicycle purchases were restricted. Gasoline in cars used for "non-essential" travel was limited to 3 gallons per week, and a wartime speed limit of 35 miles per hour was instated.

The windshield of the vehicle would display a sticker with the letter of priority ranging from A to E. A police vehicle, for instance, received an "E" sticker, as they would have no restrictions on how many gallons of gasoline they could purchase. Motorcycles were issued their own stamp, the letter "M," which meant they were allowed even less gasoline per week than a non-essential car. Furthermore, all motorcycles with the M stickers were intended for civilians on motorcycles who were involved in essential war-related activities like telegraph delivery or messenger services. The luxury of burning up rubber on motorcycle tires and letting gasoline be used for the nonsense of hill climbing became much frowned upon. Every citizen was expected to give their part toward the war effort, and motorcycle riding was seen as wasting precious resources.

The distribution of rationing books to every household began in May 1942. Rationing involved setting limits on how much a person could purchase of key grocery items such as sugar, cooking oil, coffee, cheese, bacon, etc.

Rationing books held stamps, and stamps were allocated based on a system of points awarded for each man, woman, child, and baby. Coupons were color coded, with blue coupons for processed goods and red coupons for meats. Each person started with 48 blue points and 64 red points each month. Each stamp had a number on it indicating the number of points it was worth, and a letter on it showing the rationing period it was good for.

New rationing books were issued each month. When purchasing these goods in a store, every item was posted with its point value, along with a price. Upon check-out, the consumer would need to present enough stamps for the item, then pay for it. Victory gardens were promoted, so ordinary households could can their own food and thus free up more factory-processed foods to feed the military.

Despite the restrictions, there was one event the Ghost Chasers did participate in that September of 1942, along with crowds of citizens: a "Parade of Freedom." Spencer planned this parade to be held in conjunction with the Clay County Fair ["Two Big 3-Day Events," 1942, p. 1]. The fair was not totally cancelled that year, but rather became focused on local 4-H clubs and their livestock show and sale. This would have fit in very well with the country's need to keep producing food.

The parade was planned to be held in conjunction with the events at the fairgrounds, and was to have a patriotic motif with flags of all nations, floats, patriotic organizations, the high school band, the entire *Spencer Daily Reporter* carrier staff on their bicycles, and the Ghost Chasers Motorcycle Club, among many others. In addition to the display of patriotism and support for the war effort, the parade would have a focus on children and their pets and playthings. The children of town were all invited to march at the tail end of the parade behind the floats and various parade entries and marching bands.

The parade was to be held Tuesday night, September 15, starting at 7:00 p.m. Entries in the parade were numerous and included a truck filled with scrap for the nation's war industry, a special civilian defense float, and district air raid wardens marching in a group.

"7000 Watch Parade Here Tuesday Night," exclaimed the headline in the *Spencer Daily Reporter* the day after the parade on September 16, 1942. The parade watchers packed Grand Avenue and, "various sections of the line received big applause as they passed by, including the Victory Girls and the cadets and students from the pre-glider training detachment" ["7000 Watch," 1942, p. 1]. The American Legion post members carried flags from 24 United Nations, each accompanied by a Boy Scout with a printed sign telling the country which the flag represented.

This was a town of roughly 10,000 population. What event can you imagine today where 70% of an entire town would show up?

Many special organizations for freedom participated in the parade: the Red Cross, Navy recruiting officers, the Civilian Defense unit which included the medical unit, salvage drive workers, air wardens, and the fire department. The Ghost Chasers Motorcycle Club marched, followed by the Spencer Saddle Club. Prizes were donated from the majority of the businesses in Spencer, and included such items as a bicycle tube from Montgomery Ward, a pair of Winchester roller skates from Leach and Thompson Hardware, a doll from the Bee Hive, a football from C. Ben Bjornstad Company, another football from Coast-to-Coast Store, and numerous donations of war savings stamps from many businesses.

The townspeople and their children were excited to attend, and in many cases actively participated. "Other outstanding floats included the coaster wagon pulled by two small boys in which Hitler was hung in effigy, and the other small wagon of scrap labelled, 'it's the spirit'" ["7000 Watch," 1942, p. 1].

"Dozens of pets, dogs, cats, ponies, chickens, turkeys, turtles, and even pigs were dressed in fancy costume and paraded. Some were on leashes, some in wagons, some in doll buggies, and some were carried." All of these children and animals were trailing down main street, bringing up the tail end of the glorious parade while 7000 citizens packed the sidewalks and watched. I doubt that this latter group was organized very well, say as to age of child or type of animal. And I imagine the parents had a bit of trouble corralling these children and animals at the end, much less finding them in the throngs.

The noise, the confusion, the bands playing, the cheering must all have been deafening. But what a glorious parade it was. The town of Spencer rightfully declared that "the parade was the most successful of its kind in recent history." Here in Spencer, Iowa, in 1942, children were safe and could be turned loose with all their pets at the back of a parade in a throng of people and no one thought twice about it. The enemy was a world away, where a war was raging.

And with that, the Ghost Chasers Motorcycle Club rode home and parked their bikes. The next mention of the Ghost Chasers would come in the *Milford Mail*, November 16, 1944. Mr. and Mrs. Darrell Ketcham gave a going away party for their friend, Bob Wright, who was leaving for the Navy. Several members of the Ghost Chasers and their wives attended. We would not hear from the group again until 1946.

HARLEY DAVIDSON MOTORCYCLES AND WORLD WAR II

"God didn't create metal so that man could make paper clips."

HARLEY DAVIDSON

Harley Davidson was founded in the Midwest in 1903—the factory in Milwaukee, Wisconsin is just 450 miles from Spencer. Manufacturing the first motor-driven bicycle was the brainchild of two friends who grew up just a couple of houses apart in Milwaukee: William S. Harley and Arthur Davidson. William had prior experience building bicycles while working from age 15 at the Meiselbach Bicycle Factory. He rose from the job of cycle fitter to drafter, and that led him to become a full-time draftsman at the Barth Manufacturing Company.

It was there that he developed his first internal combustion engine. He also found himself working with a childhood friend, pattern maker and draftsman Arthur, who had just designed his own pattern for a small, air-cooled gasoline engine. The two spent hours in the Davidson backyard building their first motorized bicycle, completing it in 1903. Harley was 21 years old at the time, Davidson was 22. Within a short time Walter Davidson, brother of Arthur, joined the team. He had been a bicycle racer and self-taught electrician who knew how to make his own batteries. Soon a third brother, mechanic William Davidson, joined them in their business of manufacturing motorcycles. These four young men began to rework the first prototype, designing and marketing and redesigning the motorized bicycle,e which morphed into the motorcycle in record time.

Then the Great Depression arrived, and sales of Harley Davidsons dropped from 21,000 in 1929 to less than 4000 bikes sold in 1933. The company would not have survived but for a contract to be the main supplier of motorcycles to the U. S. military. With the onset of World War II, production quickly jumped to more than 88,000 bikes as the armed forces and its allies utilized the Harley Davidson WLA models for reconnaissance, as couriers, and for general transportation of troops and supplies. The third letter of the model number, A, represents Army model. These motorcycles built for military use were 45 cubic inch flathead engines (W), and a high compression (L) model. They were sold for less than $500.00.

The war ended on September 2, 1945, and the troops were sent home. Thousands of soldiers returned home from the front wanting a bike just like they remembered riding or at least observing in the service. There was an association of wartime prestige in owning a Harley Davidson. The allure of the bike was uniquely audio, visual, and visceral. It embodied a representation of masculine thunder flying down the road with a rider aboard who felt divine freedom after the agonies of wartime.

These soldiers returning home from the war were typically single young men (the draft started at 18) who had money to spend. Though a basic private in the war was paid only about 50 dollars a month, the military provided them with their food, clothing, housing, medical needs, and even an allotment of cigarettes. What they spent overseas was minimal. It might be a 25 cent off-base haircut, a beer in a tavern, maybe a farm-baked loaf of bread, or toiletries. The rest of their pay, after spending money, was usually sent home to their families or to their banking institution and put away for when they came home. This nest egg enabled many a soldier to react to the constricts of war by buying a new motorcycle and enjoying life again.

In the case of the men who had been serving the war by managing the production of goods grown on area farms, money was good for them after the war as well. In 1947, the cost of a new car averaged $1864, the median home price was $34,500, and a new Harley Davidson Knucklehead was just under $600.

The country had struggled for ten years of the Great Depression and five years of war, and now there was a great sense of relief across the country. The pent-up demand for consumer products produced an economic boom, and the farmers were not left behind. In the United States, total farm income, after production expenses were taken out, was 3.5 billion in 1940 and rose to 15.4 billion in 1947. Times were good again, and the Midwest boys were glad to get on a newly purchased motorcycle, have some fun, maybe get a girlfriend, and ride.

Harley Davidson sales rebounded after the war. In 1946 sales were 15,554 motorcycles, most all Knuckleheads. In 1947, sales increased to 20,392—again, over half of these were Knuckleheads. In 1948, Harley Davidson had a banner year of sales, producing 31,163 motorcycles, most Panheads.

GHOST CHASERS CLUB MEMBERS–POST WORLD WAR II

Many charter members and very early members continued with the Ghost Chasers after World War II. Records show the following members active in the mid-1940s:

Early Members (mid-1940s-1950s)

Clarence Bendlin	Ray Nielson
Bob Booth	Bud Parks
Boyce Crone (Webb)	Art Rhodes
Swede Erickson	Lee Santage
Christie Albin Hansen	Ernie Singelstad
Marvin Jans	Lowell Wade
Kenny Mansfield (Sioux Rapids)	L. A. White, Jr.
Bert Mills (Webb)	Robert Wright (Everly)
Howard Nielson	Jess Young (Sioux Rapids)
Wayne Kress (Webb)	

Lee Thompson *likely member, he was a flagman at 1947 race and it is confirmed he owned a motorcycle. (*Spencer Daily Reporter, 6/27/1941*)

Gene Overeen *record not found, family reports membership

*Ghost Chasers Motorcycle Club membership card belonging to
Clarence Bendlin, signed by secretary Marvin Jans*

1946: TT RACES AT NEW DIRT OBSTACLE TRACK

The war ended in September 1945, along with rationing (with the exception of sugar). The Ghost Chasers reconvened and held their first post war event in late summer, 1946. The club sponsored motorcycle TT Races on August 25th. The races were held on a dirt track, 2 miles east of Spencer on Highway 18. This was the same area where the club had held their hill climbs prior to World War II. At this race, local Ghost Chasers members Kenny Mansfield and Jess Young from Sioux Rapids were money winners in the five-race program, entered by twelve area competition riders. There were 750 spectators at this opening of "a new dirt obstacle track" ["Local Boys Winners in TT," 1946, p. 1].

1947 RALLY IN ALGONA

The Ghost Chasers left town to join the Good Luck Motorcycle Club of Algona to stage a rally and contest at the fairgrounds on May 18, 1947. A newspaper report from the *Kossuth County Advance* told that over 350 motorcyclists from Minnesota, South Dakota, and Iowa had participated. The report said, "The track was in perfect condition and only one cyclist had a 'spill' eliminating him from an event. An egg race was the day's culminating event. There were 12 entries and Ghost Chasers member, A. L. (Lee) Santage, of Spencer, was the winner. He drove his motorcycle around the half-mile track without spilling contents of a raw egg he held on a tablespoon" ["Cycle Club Had Contest," 1947, p. 3].

1947: GHOST CHASERS ARTICLES OF INCORPORATION FILED

The Ghost Chasers Motorcycle Club filed official Articles of Incorporation with the state of Iowa in January 1947. The filing of incorporation with the Iowa Secretary of State enabled the club to gain a formal legal identity. This would have helped them with fundraising, owning club property, entering into contracts, and also could enable them to participate in some organized events. Incorporation also offered some level of protection against personal liability for club members in case of legal issues or disputes. This filing of Articles of Incorporation was no doubt necessary in order for the club to host several national AMA motorcycle races at the Clay County Fair—the first one in July, 1947.

A certified copy, dated February 11th, 1947, and shared from the collection of Paul and Sheila Currans, reads as follows:

KNOW ALL MEN BY THESE PRESENTS: That we, whose names are hereto subscribed, being of full age and citizens of the State of Iowa, and such other persons as may associate ourselves with us under these Articles of Incorporation, do hereby associate ourselves together as a body corporate, not for pecuniary profit, under and by virtue of the provisions of Chapter 394 of the 1939 Code of Iowa, and Acts amendatory thereof, assuming all powers, right, and privileges granted bodies corporate under said laws, subject only to the limitations therein provided, and do hereby adopt for ourselves, associates and successors, the following Articles of Incorporation:

Article I.
The name of this Club shall be "Ghost Chasers Cycle Club" and its principal place of business shall be at Spencer, Clay County, Iowa.

Article II.
The object of this Club shall be the promotion of cycle riding in the State of Iowa; to stimulate and maintain interest in the art of cycle riding; to obtain the best possible facilities therefor; to foster social activity and to work together for the common advantage of all who are interested in such endeavors.

Article III.

Any person, partnership, or corporation who is interested in cycle riding, is eligible to membership. To become a member, the applicant shall apply for membership to the Board of Directors and pay the membership fee.

Article IV.

This club shall have the right and power to buy, acquire, lease, and hold real estate and personal property necessary for the carrying out of the objects of the Club and shall also have the right and power to convey, rent and encumber the same. There shall be no capital stock, no dividends, no distribution of property among the members of this Club.

Article V.

The affairs of this Club shall be managed by a Board of Directors consisting of six (6) members, selected from and elected by the members at the annual meeting which shall be held on the first Monday of January of each year. These directors shall serve for a term of three (3) years or until his successor shall be duly elected and qualified. The terms of said Directors shall be so arranged that there will be two expirations each year. In the event that a vacancy should occur in the Board of Directors by resignation, disqualification, death or otherwise, during the interim between elections, it shall be filled by Board of Directors appointing a member for the un-expired portion of the term. Four Directors shall constitute a quorum to transact business.

Article VI.

The first Board of Directors of this club shall be the persons named below, each of whom shall hold such office for the term specified below, or until his successor shall be duly elected and qualified:

Robert Wright, of Everly, Iowa, shall serve until the first Monday in January, 1948;

Bert Mills of Webb, Iowa, shall serve until the first Monday in January, 1948;

Boyce Crone of Webb, Iowa shall serve until the first Monday in January, 1949;

Jess Young of Sioux Rapids, Iowa shall serve until the first Monday in January, 1949;

Ernie Singelstad of Spencer, Iowa shall serve until the first Monday in January, 1950;

Kennie Mansfield of Sioux Rapids, Iowa shall serve until the first Monday in January, 1950.

Article VII.

The officers of the Board of Directors shall consist of a President, a Vice President and a Secretary-Treasurer, who shall be elected by the Club from among their own number at the first regular meeting of the Board of Directors immediately after the annual meeting of the members each year, and each of said officers shall hold office for one (1) calendar year or until his successor shall be duly elected. The duties of such officers shall be such as may be provided for in the by-laws of this Club and such as are usually incumbent upon like corporate officers.

Until the first regular meeting of the Board of Directors in the year 1948 and until their successors shall have been duly elected, the following named Directors shall be the officers of the Board of Directors and of this Club:

Christie Hansen of Spencer, Iowa, President;
Kenny Mansfield of Sioux Rapids, Iowa, Vice-President; and
Boyce Crone of Webb, Iowa, Secretary-Treasurer

Article VIII.

The private property of the members and officers of this Club shall in no event be liable for the debts, agreements, contracts or undertakings of this Club. This Article shall never be repealed or amended.

Article IX.

This club shall have no corporate seal.

Article X.

All conveyances, contracts, agreements and obligations of this Club shall be signed by the President and Secretary-Treasurer thereof.

Article XI.

The Board of Directors of this Club shall have the following powers in addition to those otherwise set forth herein:

To make and alter by-laws for the Club which by-laws shall stand until revoked altered or amended by the Board, or by the members of the Club in meeting assembled.

To fix the membership fee or annual dues which each member of the Club shall pay and time of payment thereof.

To manage the general business and the financial affairs of the Club subject to the limitations herein expressed.

To authorize the payment of expenses that may occur in the conduct of the business.

Article XII.

The members of this club shall have the power to make, alter and amend any by-laws of the Club and may amend these Articles of Incorporation, except Article VIII hereof, by a majority vote of the members present at the annual meeting of the Club or at a special meeting of the members, providing ten days' notice in writing of such intended amendment be mailed to the members. At any such annual or special meeting or special meeting of this Club, ten (10) members will constitute a quorum for the transaction of business.

Article XIII.

The corporate period of this corporation shall begin on the date the Secretary of State issues a certificate of Incorporation, and shall terminate at the expiration of fifty (50) years from said date, with the right of renewal as provided by law, unless sooner dissolved by a majority vote of the members present at any annual meeting, or at a special meeting called for that purpose.

IN TESTIMONY WHEREOF, we have hereunto set our hands this 20, day of January A.D. 1947.

IOWA SEAL   /s/ Lorraine M. Berenger—Notary Public

/s/ Kenneth Mansfield   /s/ Robert Wright   /s/ Bert Mills

/s/ Ernie Singelstad   /s/ Jess Young   /s/ Boyce M. Crone

STATE OF IOWA, CLAY COUNTY, SS: On this 20 day of January A.D. 1947, before me, a Notary Public in and for Clay County, Iowa, personally appeared Robert Wright, Bert Mills, Boyce Crone, Jess Young, Ernie Singelstad, and Kenny Mansfield, to me personally known to be the identical persons who executed the foregoing Articles of Incorporation and acknowledged the said instrument and the execution thereof to be their voluntary act and deed for the purposes therein expressed.

WITNESS MY HAND and Notarial Seal the day and year last above written.

IOWA SEAL   /s/ Lorraine M. Berenger
                Notary Public in and for Clay County,
                State of Iowa

OFFICE OF THE SECRETARY OF STATE, Des Moines, Iowa.

This instrument recorded in Book ?-M, Page 87, January 25, 1947, Expires January 25-1947 Cert. No 2188, Receipt No. 269. Filed by B. M. Crone, Sec't., The Co., Webb, Iowa, filing fee $5.00, Recording /s/ Rollo H. Bergesen, Secretary of State.

————————————————————

Approved Jan. 25, 1947. Rollo H. Bergeson, Secretary of State.

By   /s/ C.F. O'Connor

STATE OF IOWA, COUNTY OF CLAY, SS.

I, R.B. MANN County Recorder in and for aid County, hereby certify that the above is a true copy of the Articles of Incorporation, Book C of Incorporation Records, page, 375, as the same appears of record in my office.

IN WITNESS WHEREOF, I have hereunto affixed my hand and seal. Done at my [sic] in Spencer, Iowa, this 30th day of January, A.D. 1956.

> R.B.Mann
>
> BY Naomi W. Giep, Deputy

THE NATIONAL AMA RACES AT THE CLAY COUNTY FAIRGROUNDS 1947-1950

1947 National Race

The Ghost Chasers Motorcycle Club gained tremendous attention when they sponsored their first AMA-sanctioned Half-Mile Race on Sunday, July 20, 1947, at the Clay County Fairgrounds. Even *The Sioux City Journal* advised citizens to come to Spencer and watch these AMA-sanctioned races sponsored by the Ghost Chasers Motorcycle Club.

From an original 1947 Half-Mile Race program, shared from the Clarence Bendlin collection, we learn that the Ghost Chasers Motorcycle Club was an incorporated club fully recognized by the AMA (American Motorcycle Association). This Half-Mile race was held at the Clay County Fairgrounds on their half mile oval track, which the racers would go around 8–10 times. The club hosted these races every summer for four consecutive years. The race would consist of several heats lasting 2–3 hours in duration.

The inside front page of the 1947 racing program includes the following story of the Ghost Chasers club, told in their own words:

"The Ghost Chasers Motorcycle Club was formed in 1938 with six charter members: Bob Wright, Derril Ketcham, Bernie Chestleton [sic], Dale Kabrick, and Bill Stolley.

These boys worked hard to get motorcycling started in Spencer and surrounding territory.

When World War II came along the club had 12 members but was inactive during the war while the members served in the Armed Forces and in Defense.

Our club now has 31 members besides the wives who take charge of the lunch and concessions during our different events.

We are now sponsoring a Girl Scout Troop in Spencer and hope to have a new meeting place for them soon in a new club house we are now planning.

We want to thank the Farmers Trust and Savings Bank of Spencer for allowing us to use their basement rooms for our club meetings and social get-togethers.

Our club is Incorporated under the laws of Iowa. Our riders have to abide by the rules of the American Motorcycle Association, both on and off the highway, and are rapidly making motorcycling one of the foremost pastimes for everyone.

Again, thanks for your attendance and we hope to see you at all of our events, in and out of Spencer."

Officials of the race are listed in the program on page three, Ghost Chasers members are in bold:

Judges:

Otto Ohlrecht, Sioux City   Harry Brown, Fort Dodge

Derril Ketcham, Spencer

Referee and Starter:

Robert L. Wright, Spencer   **Bud Parks,** Spencer

Secretary:

Boyce Crone, Spencer   **Lee Santage,** Spencer

Announcer:

Don Smith, Spencer

Flagmen:

Lee Thompson, Spencer   **Wayne Kress,** Spencer

Clarence Bendlin, Spencer

In Charge of Policing:

Art Rhodes, Spencer   William Roland, Spencer

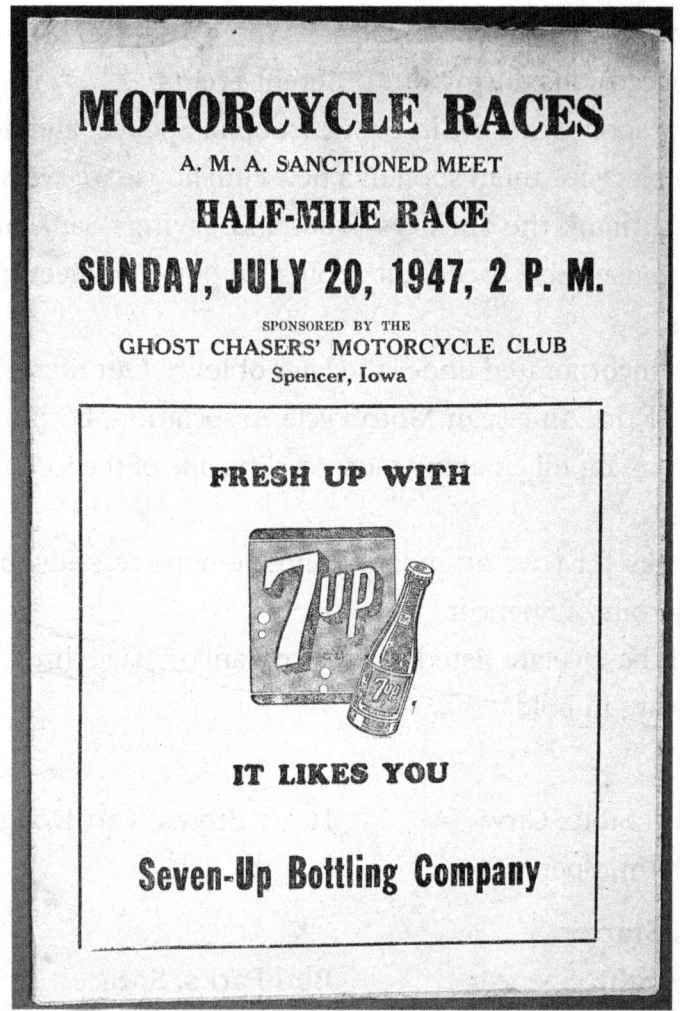

Cover of program: 1947 AMA Race held at the Clay County Fairgrounds

After the race day, the *Spencer Daily Reporter* said, "Spencer Cycle Races Thrill 3,000 Fans at Fairgrounds." It was a successful event with the only reported injury when rider Albert Swope was taken to the hospital with head injuries. Ghost Chaser member Jess Young placed 3rd in the 3-mile novice race.

Bob Bendlin, son of Ghost Chasers member Clarence Bendlin, remembers, "At the race, the judges, announcer, and flagmen went up in the flag stand. This flag stand was a platform about 10 feet tall. It was made out of steel pipe on skids with a four-sided roof made of canvas, and stairs on one side to go up. The race sponsors would move this flag stand up close to the track. At that time, the grandstand stage was mobile. In the off-season they pushed it back off the track toward the infield. This stage was made of 2×6 planks with no rails. It was about 4–5 feet high. During the motorcycle races, this stage was in the infield."

Bob remembers that his dad (Clarence Bendlin) worked at these races. In the program from July 1947, Clarence was listed as one of the three flagmen. On that day the other two flagmen were Wayne Krees [sic: Kress] and Lee Thompson.

The races were exciting and wild. Bob remembers, "The infield was *full* of bikes doing warm up or roaring back to their trailers after a race. Needless to say, it wasn't a safe place for kids to hang out. Dad would take me and Larry (younger brother), and we were just young kids—probably 3 and 5 years—and perch us up on that infield stage while the racing and roaring went on around us. He'd say, 'You're safe here. Do *not* get off this stage or I'll blister your asses.' And so we stayed put."

The race program from July 20, 1947, states that the wives of the club members handled the concession stand. A picture from the Clarence Bendlin collection shows our mom, Mary Jane Bendlin, with a group of women at the racetrack fence and all are wearing canvas aprons imprinted with "Home Lumberyard, Spencer, Iowa." We are certain she was working in the concessions stand, but could see her two boys up on that stage from where she was working across the track. The Home Lumberyard was a sponsor of the races and the women were provided with aprons to wear as their uniform when they worked the concessions stand. Sheila Currans, wife of Ghost Chasers member Paul Currans, said that usually they would serve sloppy joes, hotdogs, pop, candy bars, etc., at the concessions stand.

Bob Bendlin recalls, "The racers in these early track races wore a metal skid on their (inside) knee. They also wore a metal skid on their foot. These skids were strapped on, only on the left side, and the racers had some protection as they touched the ground going around the corners of the dirt track."

Greg White, Ghost Chasers Motorcycle Club member, recounts another story from the races at the fairgrounds. In front of the racetrack was a cement wall on the front stretch about four feet tall. This wall kept the racetrack contained and provided some protection for the audience.

Ghost Chasers wives (Margaret Santage holding sunglasses, Mary Jane Bendlin, then unknown) working concession stand. Note aprons with sponsor "Home Lumber Yard."

The race had a category of "Under 21" for younger racers to enter. In order to participate, a parent signature was required. One young man attended and forged his parent's signature enter the race. This particular young man went into a slide and hit the cement wall head on. It was the job of Ghost Chaser Club member Marvin Jans to call the young man's parents, who lived in Omaha, and inform them of their son's injury. They thought he had come to swim at the lakes and had no idea of his racing. The young man did survive his accident.

Ghost Chaser Motorcycle Club member Paul Currans remembers another time that a rider came up on the last curve, hit the cement gatepost, and got hurt pretty bad. They had to call his folks, who thought he was at a church picnic. (In reading over the old newspaper articles about the races, I found that it was common for riders to go down and get hurt. A big part of the allure of these races was that they were thrilling, with a high level of danger for the riders.)

The 1947 race had proved popular enough to warrant a repeat the following summer, but this time the club wanted it to be even bigger. They wanted to host a National Race. To do this they would need permission from not only the fairgrounds, but from the American Motorcycle Association racing group.

1948 National Race

It was springtime, 1948, and the Ghost Chasers set out to put their plans of hosting a larger AMA National Race into motion. On April 8, club members met at the Kenny Mansfield home in Sioux Rapids to discuss plans for a three-mile national race. The report says that the president of the club is Kenny Mansfield, and the secretary/treasurer is Art Rhodes ["Ghost Chasers Make Plans for National Race," 1948 p. 1].

The *Sioux City Journal* from April 14, 1948, tells that "Spencer Planning Three New Athletic Enterprises." A group from the Ghost Chasers Motorcycle Club of Spencer met with the fair directors to obtain permission to use the half-mile track for the national motorcycle races sanctioned by the AMA. "The fair board intimated the races would be held if satisfactory dates could be arranged" ["Spencer Planning," 1948, p. 34].

In the *Sioux City Journal* April 21, 1948, the headline states, "Set Motorcycle Races at Spencer June 27" and reports that a special three-mile motorcycle race sanctioned by the American Motorcycle Association has been scheduled for Sunday, June 27, on the half-mile oval track at the Clay County Fairgrounds. Nine events would be included in the program sponsored by the Ghost Chasers Motorcycle Club.

An advertisement was found in the Sioux Rapids Bulletin Press published on June 24, 1948. Citizens were advised to come see "Thrills and Spills" at the National 3 Mile Motorcycle Championship Race. Time trials were to start at

10:00 a.m., and then the races would commence at 2:00 p.m. The program includes nine other races for amateurs, experts, and novices.

Unfortunately, this well-advertised national championship race, which would be attended by thousands, hit a serious snag when the event had to be cancelled due to severe thunderstorms. Two solid days of rain caused the track to be mud. The club was somewhat undeterred and decided that a postponement to a Monday race would allow the sun to dry the track enough to race.

The majority of the racers remained in Spencer another night, and those who opted to leave were scratched from the AMA association. Bob Wright, spokesperson for the Ghost Chasers, told the public that all of the top-notch racers who had filed entry blanks were in town and anxious to get out on the track and iron out the bugs. He said that after they were allowed to ride the oval and get a feel for the track conditions, they would be changing sprocket sizes and getting ready for racing ["Races This Afternoon," 1948, p. 5].

It was on a Monday in the daytime when the postponed races were held. One can only imagine the size of the crowd if the races could have been held on a Sunday as originally planned. As it was, 2500 citizens gathered in the stands to cheer for the racers. An article in the *Spencer Daily Reporter* printed an article by sportswriter Bob Mackey. His introduction was fabulous: "After the dust had settled and the oil and special fuel mixture fumes had blown away yesterday at the local fairgrounds, one thing was reasonably certain to the 2500 people gathered there. If you want to live to a ripe old age, don't take up motorcycle racing" ["Anthony Tops Riders," 1948, p. 7].

Leo Anthony of Port Huron, Michigan, won the National Three Mile Championship race, proudly accepting the gold- and cream-colored trophy. There were flawless riding abilities shown—along with three spills which marred the race. However, no one was reported to have suffered any significant injuries.

Greg White remembers one of the National Races held by the Ghost Chasers in the 1940s. There were clubs in attendance from all over the country and Canada. There was a huge audience. He remembers walking the track with Ghost Chasers club member and local motorcycle shop owner Ernie Singelstad early on the day of the race. He was about seven years old. He and Ernie, along with a couple other young boys, walked the track to pick up any stones that might fly up and hit the racers.

1949 National Race

Bob Wright, president of the Ghost Chasers Motorcycle Club, announced in the *Sioux Rapids Bulletin Press* that this year's 1949 Half-Mile Flat Track race was going to be one of the largest ever held in Northwest Iowa. The location was again at the Clay County Fairgrounds half-mile racetrack. Scheduled for Memorial Day, the May 30th race began with time trials at 11:00 a.m. and official racing starting at 2:00 p.m. There were nine events, just as last year, and there was a $12,000 purse up for grabs.

The race was designated as a Class C race. Bob Wright explained that 75–100 entrants were expected, one of the racers being local favorite and Ghost Chasers member Jess Young from Sioux Rapids ["Jess Young to Race," 1949, p. 1].

1950 National Race

The Clay County Fairgrounds was once again the site of the fourth annual National Motorcycle Classic sanctioned by the AMA, sponsored by the Ghost Chasers and held on Memorial Day weekend: Tuesday, May 30, 1950. Five thousand people crowded the bleachers and track area to be "served up a dish of thrills, spills, and dust," according to the write-up in the *Spencer Daily Reporter*. The entire program included heat races of six laps and finals of eight laps in three divisions—novice, amateur, and expert.

With colorful sports writing so typical of the time period, readers were somewhat shocked with the news that "No less than five daredevil riders were injured to make the affair appear more like a suicide excursion than a legitimate contest. This report, in fact, will read more like a traffic fatality list than a straight sports report" ["Five Injured in Motorcycle Racers," 1950, p. 2]. The injuries were listed: "Joe Holondek of Omaha fractured a rib; Bill Merwald of Omaha was treated for a fractured right leg, broken jaw, and shock; Lawrence Lowe of West Des Moines was treated for a fractured finger, face lacerations and shock; Dale Shafer from Omaha was treated for a broken left collarbone, head injuries, shock; and Clif Edwards from Grand Island, Nebraska, was treated for a bruised right knee. All of them were transported to the Spencer Municipal Hospital for their treatment."

Ghost Chasers Motorcycle Club member Jess Young of Sioux Rapids, a local favorite in this race but referred to in the article as "a real old-timer in motorcycle racing circles," failed to qualify for a spot in the expert finals—he came in fourth in the first qualifying heat. In order to qualify for the finals in each division, the racer needed to come in one of the first three places in the heat. The other qualification was that "their bodies remain intact" ["Five Injured in Motorcycle Races," 1950, p. 2]. The winner of the expert final race was Johnny Egeberg from Minneapolis. His eight-lap time was 4:27:89.

We don't know why this was the last National Motorcycle Classic race that the Ghost Chasers sponsored. It surely wasn't for lack of interest. Quite possibly it was due to the number of injuries sustained and the track conditions. There is mention of a large amount of dust at this race, which means that visibility could have certainly been a factor for the racers, leading to highly dangerous conditions. In the midst of dust clouds on the track, riders are blind to what is right in front of them and crashes are likely. In the modern racing events, tracks must be watered down to prevent too much dust. Another reason may be that the popularity of these races had grown to the point that they needed larger facilities. In any case, all we know is that this was the last National Motorcycle Classic race held at the Clay County Fair Grounds.

ERNIE SINGELSTAD AND THE SPENCER CYCLE SHOP

Probably the single most influential person responsible for the popularity of motorcycles in Spencer was Ghost Chasers early club member Ernie Singelstad (1916–2003), who owned the Spencer Cycle Shop. His business was located at three different locations between 1945 and 1956, each move made in order to improve the storefront and showroom.

Born in Northwood, Iowa, Ernie graduated high school there in 1934, and went on to a master mechanics school in Los Angeles, California. In 1936 he returned home to Northwood to work in the contracting business with his dad, Andrew Singelstad. In his early years, Ernie had become quite skilled in carpentry, working alongside his father building not only homes but huge barns that still dot the countryside in Worth County, Iowa [Touring Singelstad Barns, 2023. P.6].

Shortly after returning home from Los Angeles to begin work with his father, Ernie had a motorcycling adventure that Bob Bendlin remembered: "Ernie worked the very first Sturgis race. Somehow, they knew of Ernie and got ahold of him and wanted him to come help. He was quite young for a trip of that distance, but his mom threw sandwiches in the saddle bag of his motorcycle and he left early that next morning, riding non-stop to get to Sturgis that same night."

The roads from Northwood, Iowa to Sturgis in 1937 were not easy interstates. In fact, I-90 wasn't finished until 1976. It was still the Depression years, and though there had been an infusion of labor during the 1930s for Depression-era job creation programs which included road building, their work was far from complete. There was no direct route for Ernie to make this trip, but rather he would have used rough two-lane highways when available, along with dirt or gravel roads in places to navigate to connecting roads.

The distance he traveled that day on his motorcycle was around 575 miles. This was the same year that Amelia Earhart disappeared over the Pacific Ocean, the same year that the Hindenburg exploded while trying to dock in New Jersey, and just ten years after the carving of Mount Rushmore had begun. And there was Ernie, hell bent for Sturgis, riding a motorcycle manufactured in the early 1930s, no doubt a Harley Davidson of very early model, determined to get to those races by nightfall.

According to Ernie's daughter Joyce Freeman, he made that trip to Sturgis to take part in the very first unofficial race that the JackPine Gypsies held there in 1937. After this first practice year, they held their first official rally in Sturgis the following year, calling it the Black Hills Motor Classic in August of 1938. This rally was sponsored by the JackPine Gypsies Motorcycle Club, which still holds this yearly rally and owns the tracks, hill climb, and field areas where the rally is centered.

After four years working with his father in the construction business, Ernie took a position as installation superintendent for the Horn Manufacturing Company in Fort Dodge. It was 1940 and the country was gearing up for the approaching war. During World War II, Ernie worked installing folding hangars for the war effort and supervised jobs in 40 states, Mexico, and Canada.

After the war, Ernie moved to Spencer on July 1, 1945, to establish himself as a carpenter. When the war ended in 1945, the housing market had begun to grow astronomically across the country as G.I.s returned home and started families. Ernie had identified Spencer as a town where he could make money using his skills in carpentry to build new homes as well as a place to compete with his motorcycle. Within three months he was granted a Harley Davidson dealership and opened his first Spencer Cycle Shop about October 1, 1945. It was located in a garage at 119 West 14th Street. He was a skilled mechanic and was able to offer parts and repair of most all types of motorcycles as well.

On May 1, 1946, Ernie married Beulah Carroll in Fort Dodge. She joined him in Spencer, where he had begun to build their first home on the same property as his shop: 119 West 14th Street. This home was completed in 1948.

Ernie and Beulah Singelstad outside the Harley Davidson factory in Milwaukee. They went to pick up a new K Model for the Clay County Fair. (Photo courtesy of Singelstad family)

For the next several years he continued to have the dual career of building homes and running his Harley Davidson dealership. During this time, he built at least five homes for Spencer families as well as his own home and shop within just a few years of arriving in Spencer. Though carpentry was a skill that earned him a living to support his growing family during those early years, his first and primary interest was always motorcycles. Ernie had been a motorcycle enthusiast from his teenaged years. He rode motorcycles, he raced motorcycles, and he competed in hill climbs. During the summer months, he toured the motorcycle circuit for hill-climbing and half-mile race competition from about 1945 to 1956 with his young wife, Beulah, cheering him on.

In 1948 Ernie relocated the Spencer Cycle Shop to its second location about a block east of the South "T" (but on the north side of the road) at the junction of Highway 71 and Highway 18. This building had been an old gas station prior to his occupancy. In the summer of 1949, he strategically added Schwinn bicycles to his showroom and offered sales as well as bicycle repair.

Ernie Singelstad's second Spencer Cycle Shop located at "South T"
in Spencer. (Photo courtesy of the Singelstad family)

Bob Bendlin remembers a story about Ernie that happened right at that time. It illustrates the enthusiasm Ernie had for the Harley Davidson motorcycles. He said, "After Ernie had his motorcycle shop, Harley Davidson came out with a new model in 1948, the Panhead V-Twin. Ernie wanted one real bad to display in his showroom, and he knew he had to go to the factory in Milwaukee, Wisconsin, to pick it up. He had an old bike which he rode to

Milwaukee, leaving early in the morning. Once there, he left the old bike and got the new bike, then turned right around to make the trip back to Spencer.

"By then it was dark, and Ernie was crossing the bridge in La Crosse over the Mississippi (probably Highway 16, which spans 2,573 feet) when the headlight fell off the new bike. He had to get stopped on that bridge in the pitch black, and get the light reattached and working before he could proceed. This was a scare he never forgot. He figured that they had just forgotten to tighten the headlight bolts down at the factory."

Today the 456-mile trip driving a car from Spencer, Iowa to Milwaukee, Wisconsin, is estimated at seven and a half hours one way. This modern Trip Advisor estimate is calculated driving on today's interstates and highways—no doubt a much quicker trip than the one Ernie took in 1948. Ernie did this on a motorcycle that had little value and was beat up enough that he intended to leave it behind. When he arrived, he completed the transaction, ditched the old bike, turned around and drove the same distance home again on the brand new Panhead—which he had never ridden before—in the dark.

Ernie's daughter, Joyce Freeman, shared that her dad returned to Milwaukee on another trip to purchase the very first K-series Harley Davidson off the production line around 1952.

Sometime between March 1948 and September 1949, Ernie applied for and received a permit to erect a brand-new shop out of block, for a cost of $1500.00. The permit address for this third Spencer Cycle Shop was listed as 18 West 4th Street Southwest, a two-story red brick shop that faced the river—now West Leach Park. He then expanded by building an attached one-story building to the east side, which had an adjoining address of 14 West 4th Street Southwest.

The new addition became his main storefront. He held a grand opening on March 1, 1951, and it seems that the city had combined the two addresses into a new one—calling the location 20 West 4th Street Southwest, according to a newspaper clipping shared by Ernie's daughter Joyce Freeman ["Know Your Business Men," 1951, p.?]. This third shop was not far from Grand Avenue (Highway 71), near where the Dairy Queen is located. Ernie and his family lived in a small house behind this shop, facing the next street over on 5th Street Southwest, which also faced the rear of the Dairy Queen.

Group of Ghost Chasers Motorcycle Club members lined up in front of Spencer Cycle Shop, owned by Ernie Singelstad. (Photo courtesy of the Singelstad family and Greg White)

A story about Ernie at a hill climb in Sioux Rapids was shared by Ernie's daughter, Joyce Freeman. She wrote, "Mom and Dad went to a hill climb in the late 1940s where dad hurt his ankle. He couldn't drive them home with that ankle, and Mom had never driven a car before, but Dad taught her how to drive that day to get home from Sioux Rapids, pulling the trailer with his motorcycle loaded in it! And the car was a stick shift! He told that story a lot."

Both Bob Bendlin and Greg White recall a story about Ernie when he was interviewed by local radio announcer Mason Dixon in 1947 at the half-mile race. The interview was broadcast live from the fairgrounds and Ernie's slow, measured way of talking must have been a little frustrating for the fast-talking radio announcer on live airspace. In Greg's words: "Ernie talked real slow—you had to drive stakes to see if he was moving, and it's just the way it was. And when they had these races in 1947 at the fairgrounds, the local station, which was KICD, and the famous announcer, as you know, was Mason Dixon. Well, Mason Dixon interviewed Ernie for the races and that got all done, and they shut off the mic, and he says, 'Ernie, you're a great guy, you're a good family man, you're a good dealer, you're an asset to the community, but I'm going to tell you one thing—you'll never be a radio announcer—so you keep doing what you're doing!' And it was Ernie who told me that story and everyone got a big kick out of that—including Ernie."

Greg White continues, "Regarding the 1947 motorcycle races at the Clay County Fairgrounds, that was a big deal. It was, I believe, a National Championship—and I can remember there were clubs of motorcyclists that came to watch, some of them even from Canada. So anyway, I thought I was pretty important at seven years old and Ernie Singelstad, the Harley dealer, had me walk around with him and a couple other boys picking up all the rocks off the track so they wouldn't go up and hit the riders in the nose or eyes, you know."

Ernie's racing bike (photo courtest of Singelstad family, G. White)

Greg remembered visiting Ernie's shop on 4th Street Southwest as a teenager—one time with a good friend, Gary Easton (Gary was the son of early Ghost Chasers member Ralph Easton). In Greg's words, "At that time the surface of that street was gravel, it was not a paved street. And I think I had a Matchless (motorcycle) then and Gary Easton, a good friend of mine, a cycle nut, had a—I believe a—German one. And Ernie says, 'We gotta see which one of you guys is fastest, you know, line 'em up out here!' So, we thought that was real cool. So, we lined 'em up in front of the shop going west, you know, and somebody dropped their handkerchief, the flag, and away we went you know, and I don't remember who was ahead, but we went to turn around, and there was a city police car—right crossways across the street. And I came close to peeing in my pants. But we talked to them, and they let us go."

Greg explained that kids would get a learner's permit to drive at age 14, which was intended to be used driving with your parents in the car while you learned to drive. Instead, he and many of his friends took a lenient view of the learner's permit and thought that since a motorcycle was for a single passenger, they were free to use that learner's permit to drive a motorcycle anywhere with no parent around. Today learner's permits are still issued to fourteen-year-olds by the Iowa Motor Vehicle Division. The modern rules allow one to drive a motorcycle with this learner's permit, but the supervising parent or guardian must be within sight and hearing of the motorcycle and be on or in a different vehicle. A parent or guardian can also give written permission to another adult who is at least 25 years of age.

Greg had another story about Ernie that tells quite a bit about his character, kindness, and patience toward others. Greg said, "When I was 14, I had an oil system failure on my Harley and that's when I met Jeff's dad (Marvin Jans). I was pushing my bike a mile east of Fostoria because I had a cousin who was real good to me (and would help) and Marv (Jans) and his dad pulled up beside me and said, 'We'll get it going for you!' and then they did, you know. So anyway then in the spring, sitting out in the yard in my very primitive garage accommodations, I pulled the cylinders off at 14 and I took them down to Ernie's and he honed them out for larger pistons, and he says, 'Now, Greg', he says, 'I'll come over tonight and help you put those pistons inside the cylinders and on the bike,' and he says, 'It's pretty tricky, and... I'll do that.' So he came over and he looked at it and he said, 'Well, you have it ready to go except for one thing.' He said, 'It's not clean enough. You've gotta clean this and this and this and this. And I'll be over tomorrow and help you' (put the pistons in). And he did that. I thought that was pretty nice of him and it was my first experience at cleanliness."

In 1953, Spencer experienced a major flood which destroyed many homes and businesses, including the Spencer Cycle Shop. This flood was equally as bad as the flood of 2024 and many similarities have been made of the two. Clarence Bendlin took his boat down to Ernie's shop and the two of them worked tirelessly to evacuate many people. Ernie's daughter Joyce Freeman remembered stories about this and shared that her dad felt that it was important to always help out neighbors in need. His own shop was knee deep in water, but other folks needed him.

Ernie Singelstad on his racing motorcycle.
Photo courtesy of the Singelstad family and Greg White

Ernie Singelstad at Hill Climb (Photo courtesy of the Singelstad family and Greg White)

1954 may have been Ernie's last year of racing his motorcycle. Annual Memorial Day Races were held at the Okoboji Speed Bowl on May 30, 1954. The races were sponsored by the Ghost Chasers Motorcycle Club. The *Spencer Daily Reporter* says that the six fastest riders in the timed trials included Ernie Singelstad of Spencer. There were riders from South Dakota, New York, Minnesota, and Iowa [Four Wins Scored, 1954, p. ?]. Ernie was 38 years old.

In 1956, Ernie closed the Spencer Cycle Shop. Whether due to losses from the flood which he could never recover from, or the competition from so many foreign motorcycles that were flooding the market, it was time to give it up. The family stayed in Spencer until springtime 1957, moving to a farm near Langdon where Ernie farmed. Joyce Freeman shared that after the family moved to the farm, he had a lot of guys with motorcycles stopping by for repairs. Ernie always helped them. He also continued to do carpentry, usually building a home every winter.

In 1973 Ernie and his family relocated again, this time moving to Terril. Ernie worked in lumber yards and remodeled many homes in and around Terril until his retirement. He even served as the town mayor of Terril for a number of years in the 1980s. After Ernie's death in 2003, the family took comfort knowing that Ernie's life legacy was that "He helped whenever someone had a need."

Ernie up on one wheel (photo courtesy of Singelstad family, G. White)

Ernie racing (photo courtesy of Singelstad family, G. White)

GHOST CHASERS MOTORCYCLE CLUB MEMBER CLARENCE BENDLIN

Clarence Bendlin was a longstanding member of the Ghost Chasers, belonging to the club for over ten years during the club's "heyday" in the 1940s and 1950s. Like so many of the other members of the Ghost Chasers, he was a part of the farming community in Clay County. His maternal great-grandparents, Michael and Amelia Bernhagen, had homesteaded their farm east of Langdon in 1871. This farm stayed in the Bernhagen family for over 100 years. His paternal grandparents, William and Mathilde Bendlin, immigrated from Germany in the 1800s and also made their way to settle into farming life in Clay County. Clarence was born to Gus and Ruth (Bernhagen) Bendlin at a farm near Spencer on September 1, 1922.

He grew up during the Golden Age of tractors (1920s-1940s) when an agricultural revolution, sparked by Ford's first mass-produced affordable tractor in 1917, induced farmers to transition from their horse-pulled plows to gas-driven machinery of all types. Clarence knew engines well, and he especially knew motorcycles. By the time he was thirteen years old, he had begun earning spending money doing farm work alongside his dad, Gus, taking their farm machinery to neighboring farms to help others with harvest.

Gus owned a threshing machine for harvesting oats, a corn sheller with steel wheels, and an automated baler that produced bales bound with wire which needed to be manually tied off. All of these machines called for quite a few men to work as a team on and around the machines to accomplish the jobs they were designed to do.

At twelve years of age, it was common for boys to be doing manual labor on the farms, and Clarence was no exception. The various neighbors whom they helped included Ruth's brother, Earl Bernhagen, Ray Lawrence and his brother, Roy Lawrence, and Louis Hansen, who all lived on neighboring farms near Langdon.

It would not have taken long before Clarence had saved up enough money to purchase his first Harley Davidson motorcycle. We know from family stories that he rode this motorcycle to school at Lake Center when he was a teenager. Lake Center School was just a few miles from the Bendlin farm.

In the Clarence Bendlin collection, the original registration paper of his first motorcycle provides us with interesting information.

CERT. OF REG. MOTORCYCLE 1945, State of Iowa
REGIS. NO.
Owner: Clarence Bendlin   21-597
Street or R.F.D.
P.O.: Spencer
Date of Reg. 1/4/45   Times Reg. 10
Make: Harley Davidson   Date of Poss. 1935
Model: Fee: $2.50
Year: 1935   Penalty:
Motor No. 35VLD5255   Total:
Prev. Reg. No. 548
Signature of Owner: *Clarence Bendlin*

Motorcycle registration for 1935 Harley Davidson

Clarence Bendlin on 1935 Harley Davidson, location Spencer

What does "Motor No. 35VLD5255" mean? Harley Davidson had a precise way of imprinting the VIN number on its motorcycles. The first two numbers indicated the year the bike came off the production line—35 denoted the year 1935. The next set of three letters indicated the model designation. The VL series was made between 1930–1936. The letter V indicates that the motorcycle was a flathead V-twin. (Harley Davidson manufactured both a 74 and an 80 cubic inch side-valve V-twin engine). The letter L meant the engine was high compression.

The last letter in the group of three letters denoted one of the following (only three choices): The letter D meant the motorcycle had increased **D**isplacement. The letter A meant it had been manufactured for the **A**rmy. The third possibility was the letter R, which would mean a factory **R**acer. Further, if the letter combination ended in D, the motorcycle was powered by the 74 cubic inch flathead V-twin paired with a hand-shifted 3 speed transmission.

The last set of numbers indicated the exact number in the production line of this particular motorcycle. Thus, this motorcycle owned by Clarence was a 1935 VL series bike with a 74 cubic inch high compression flathead V-twin engine paired with a hand shifted three speed transmission, built with increased displacement for increased performance, and was bike number 5255 off the production line at the Harley Davidson factory.

Mary Jane Bendlin

This registration paper shows Clarence registered this motorcycle in 1945, and the form says it has been registered 10 times. That fits, since it is a 1935 motorcycle. But then the form says "date of possession" and the year 1935 is again filled in. We know that Clarence owned a motorcycle as a teenager and rode it to school. It is hard to believe that he has owned this motorcycle since 1935, as he was only 13 years old in 1935. He was the oldest child in the family, so it could not have belonged to an older sibling. It is unlikely that his father rode the motorcycle. This is a family mystery that will probably never be solved.

In any case, we are certain that he began riding his motorcycle to school as a teenager. This 1935 motorcycle was probably sold right before the purchase of the brand new 1947 Knucklehead from Ernie Singelstad.

Clarence Bendlin married Mary Jane Freeburg on May 29, 1943. Like so many couples in Spencer, Iowa, in the 1940s, they no doubt met in town on a Friday night. Possibly it was at a street dance, and quite possibly he offered her a ride on his first Harley Davidson. In any case, they both enjoyed riding motorcycles, and fun-loving Mary Jane accompanied him on most of his rides during their early married years. They spent their lives farming northeast of Spencer and raising their four children.

Clarence Bendlin on Black Hills trip

Clarence in motorcycle riding gear. Note kidney belt.

Clarence on motorcycle trip, stopping at "Welcome to Minnesota" state line

THE HARLEY DAVIDSON KNUCKLEHEAD

Bob Bendlin remembers, "Ernie Singelstad was a lifelong friend of our dad, Clarence Bendlin. Clarence bought a brand new 1947 H.D. Knucklehead EL from Ernie's shop. It was the second motorcycle he owned, and would have been quite an upgrade."

It had a 61 cubic inch EL "hemi" overhead valve engine, with a 4-speed gearbox. Nicknamed the Knucklehead due to the distinctive shape of the rocker boxes, which resembled the knuckles of a closed fist, it was Harley's first fully overhead valve street engine. It also came with a speedometer as standard equipment and claimed a top speed of 90 MPH.

The EL featured a springer front suspension. The rear wheel had no suspension, giving this type of motorcycle another nickname: the hardtail. The Knucklehead was only manufactured until 1947 and was replaced by the Panhead engine in 1948. Over 11,000 Knuckleheads were sold in 1947, which made up over half of H.D. total sales of 20,000 bikes.

The Knucklehead EL was the "hot version":

- 40 HP
- Carburetion: 1.25" Linkert
- Primary: chain
- Transmission: 4-speed
- Hand shift/ foot clutch
- Springer forks, rigid rear
- 59.5 inch wheelbase
- Weight: 565 pounds dry
- MSRP: $590.00

Receipts show that Clarence Bendlin paid more than $700 for his new 1947 Knucklehead, but that would have included extra accessories—factory saddlebags, tool kit, etc.

TRIPS ON THE 1947 HARLEY DAVIDSON KNUCKLEHEAD

We know from a souvenir racing program and family stories that Ghost Chasers member Clarence Bendlin's first long-distance trip was riding his new 1947 Harley Davidson Knucklehead to the Daytona Beach National in March 1948 with fellow motorcycle rider Jack Ihri of Royal. They left from Spencer very early in March in bitter cold weather conditions. He wore a pair of sheepskin-lined gloves that went up over his wrists onto his upper arms. He later talked about how they rode straight through with no stops—four hundred or so miles south—until they reached far into Missouri and the weather warmed up enough for him to take off those gloves.

The trip was one that many people today would call "the trip of a lifetime." It became a trip that he always recalled with a smile and shake of his head that they had actually gone so far and done such a thing on those older model Harleys. He had so much fun that mom joined him the following year, but this time they went by car to the Daytona Beach race in 1949.

Daytona hosted a 200-mile road race, which was billed as "the Kentucky Derby of Motorcycledom." From an official program from the event, we learned that over 178 veteran riders competed in the AMA National Championship Race in the expert category on Thursday, March 11, 1948. Part of the race was on the beach, and part was along Highway A1A. Mom noted on the program, "Clarence and Mary Bendlin went berserk (sic) during this race." She also noted on the cover that Dick Klamforth was the 1949 champion.

Members of the Ghost Chasers Motorcycle Club frequently made trips to the Black Hills area of South Dakota. Clarence Bendlin, often accompanied by Mary Jane, would make these trips with one or two other couples on motorcycles. Rapid City was a distance of about 450 miles from Spencer, and the group would often take rest stops along their route. One popular place to stop along the way was at Wall Drug Store, famous since the 1930s for advertising a cold drink to weary travelers. Once at their destination, the couples could stay at one of the many available camping sites in the area or they could rent a room for a night or two.

Clarence Bendlin's souvenir buckle from Daytona Motorcycle Race

The Black Hills take their name from the Lakota who called them Paha Sapa, which means "hills that are black." The hills lend a colorful contrast to the South Dakota highways, which are pink in color due to deposits of Sioux Quartzite, as old as two billion years.

A famous road for motorcyclists to travel in the Black Hills was the Iron Mountain Road, with its pigtail bridges built by the Civilian Conservation Corps (CCC) in 1933. The Iron Mountain Road is seventeen miles long, with 314 curves through pine and deciduous forests and historic tunnels. In addition, Mount Rushmore was completed in 1941 and was a very popular destination, as well as the Badlands National Park.

The most famous destination for motorcyclists was the Sturgis Motorcycle Rally, held every year in early August. Members of the Ghost Chasers Motorcycle Club were was frequent attendees.

Clarence Bendlin, Mary Jane Bendlin, Phyllis Booth (Mrs. Bob Booth) on Black Hills trip

Motorcycle riding was considered great fun for the women, and Mary Jane Bendlin is seen in many photos sitting atop dad's motorcycle. She loved riding, whether it was just a spin into town to ride up and down main street on a Saturday night or taking a road trip.

It was very common for wives or girlfriends to hop on the back of the motorcycles and ride with the men. The women usually wore a canvas cap, or "scull-cap," to keep their hair in place while riding. Men wore these rather than helmets as well. Our mom, Mary Jane, kept three such caps in various colors. These caps were tight-fitting, similar to a bathing cap, but had longer sides and a snap to fasten under the chin. Women often wore motorcycle goggles similar to the men's, in those days made with Eisenglass lenses.

*Trip line-up: Clarence and Mary Jane Bendlin, Phyllis and
Bob Booth, Lee Santage with daughter Sharon*

Mary Jane Bendlin and Phyllis Booth on board

During World War II, women had begun to wear pants, popularized by Katherine Hepburn and Marlene Dietrich in films, but also due to their practicality. Women who worked in the factories and helped out with other male dominated jobs during the war found pants allowed them easier movement. This fashion trend continued after the war, and the loose trouser style pants allowed women freedom to hop on the back of a motorcycle and enjoy the sport.

Wives of Ghost Chasers members: Mary Jane Bendlin (Mrs. Clarence Bendlin), Lila Merchant (Mrs. Bud Parks), and Margaret Santage (Mrs. Lee Santage)

The suspension on the bikes was pretty rough, with no rear shock absorbers, and the heat and humidity of the Midwest summers after endless miles going down the road and getting whipped in the face could take a toll. Our mom, Mary Jane Bendlin, was a trooper and loved a good time. She went with our dad, Clarence, on many motorcycle trips.

Lila Merchant (Mrs. Bud Parks) and Mary Jane Bendlin (Mrs. Clarence Bendlin)

On the trip that I believe was her last extended vacation on a motorcycle, Mary Jane and Clarence—along with good friends and fellow Ghost Chasers Motorcycle Club members Bob and Phyllis Booth—traveled on a motorcycle vacation to the Black Hills. This was before the interstates we travel on today had been built, and I believe their route would have been the Old U.S. Highway 16. From Sioux Falls this route became difficult, with rougher surfaces and steeper grades and winding roads, but scenic.

Mom had not been feeling well, and this was no doubt the reason that on the way home they had decided to go south to Nebraska to get on a straighter and faster route. Phyllis wrote a letter in 1993, remembering their harrowing trip: "Going through Nebraska it was so hot that day. We stopped and Mary was sick from heat stroke. She layed (sic) down and didn't want to go on. Clarence called her an old sheep and said all she wanted to do was lay down & die like a sheep. Needless to say, he had her on the fight then." His goading gave her the gumption to get up, climb back on the bike, and they were able to go on.

Bob Bendlin recalls that as mom lay there on the side of the road dad had said to her, "You have two choices. You can lay here and die like an old sheep or you can get back on this bike." This may seem like a harsh thing to say, but to his credit he was probably being truthful. On these trips in the late 1940s–early 1950s, there were no highway rest stops and few places for a cold drink. There was little traffic and no help, no cell phone, no way out but to keep on going.

The "suitcase" of belongings for the couple riding on the motorcycle would have to fit inside the bike's saddlebags along with the tool kit. Mom recalled that trip many times over the years, remembering how terribly ill she was from heatstroke. Always after that, she was very sensitive to staying in the heat very long.

Though these longer motorcycle trips slowed during the years, our dad, Clarence Bendlin, rode his Knucklehead to the Clay County Fair every year in the fall. This went on from the time he bought it well into the 1960s. He worked with the stage crew for many years and then later moved to Gate C, where he enjoyed his job taking tickets and seeing so many people he knew.

Many other friends and motorcycle club members also rode their bikes to the fair in the fall. Upon entering Gate C, I recall seeing the Harleys all parked in a row just to the south of the gate inside the fairgrounds.

After dad stopped riding his Harley to the fair, he continued to work every fall at the fair. Like so many of his generation who worked at the fair, it was not for the money but rather for the social experience of meeting up with old friends who never missed attending the fair in the fall. Altogether, Clarence Bendlin worked at the Clay County Fair for over 40 years.

GHOST CHASERS ANTICS

While the Ghost Chasers professed to be upstanding and law abiding, sponsoring a Girl Scout Club, they still enjoyed their fun on the motorcycles and a bit of "hell-raising" was done. A few citizens were mildly upset at their antics. Floyd Breidinger told Bob, "Those boys were raising hell in town (on Saturday night) and cops weren't doing anything about it. The cops would go to one end of town and the motorcycles took off before they got there. They would just go back and forth like that all night, up and down Main."

Bob Bendlin recalls, "Club members would ride together and go to town—ride up and down Main in a pack, raised hell, spun gravel. They would go from Swanson's (where Slumberland Furniture is now located south of town) and then go to Richie's. Richie's is at the site where Hy-Vee is today, and the Maid-Rite café was at the front corner of that lot. There they would turn around and make that loop again and again."

Sidenote: At the north end of the Swanson's store was the Villager hamburger stand. It sold the first fast food in Spencer—hamburgers cost 15 cents. My thought is that they were going from one hamburger/milkshake joint back to the other. These places would have been popular gathering spots for townspeople on Saturday night.

In the Clarence Bendlin collection of Ghost Chasers Motorcycle Club memorabilia, there is a handmade metal badge, approximately 5" by 3", with a large safety pin attachment soldered on the back. The pin is black with yellowing painted letters which say, **"Ghost Chasers Mcy. C.,"** followed by a center larger printed line, **"I'M A SISSY"** and a third line, **"I FELL OFF."** This badge was passed around to fellow Ghost Chasers members who had the misfortune of taking a spill from their bike. It was to be worn on their jacket as a badge of shame until they could pass it on to the next member who tipped their bike over. This badge is an example of the good-natured teasing and practical jokes that were a part of the club. The members enjoyed each other's company and were always out for a good time.

Just for fun: Ghost Chasers Motorcycle Club members passed this around to the member who took a spill from their bike

The back of "I'm A Sissy" pin

Goggles worn by Clarence Bendlin: "NYD Resistal" retail $3.50.
Non-shatterable, aviation type with sponge rubber binding.

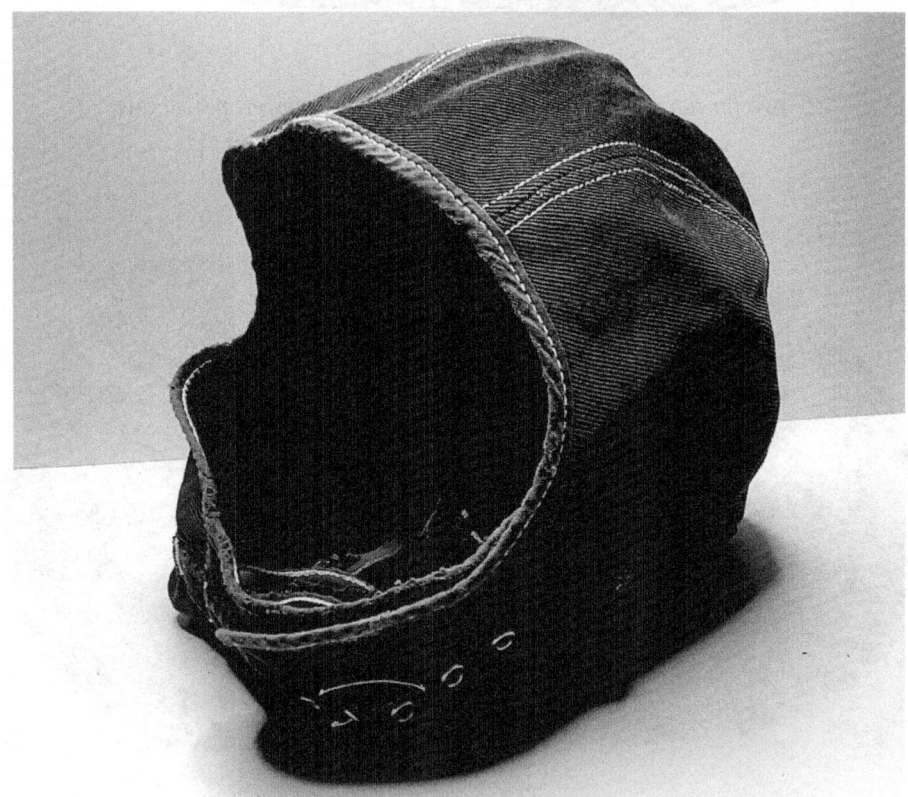

Canvas cap worn by Mary Jane Bendlin

1953 Gypsy Tour belt buckle

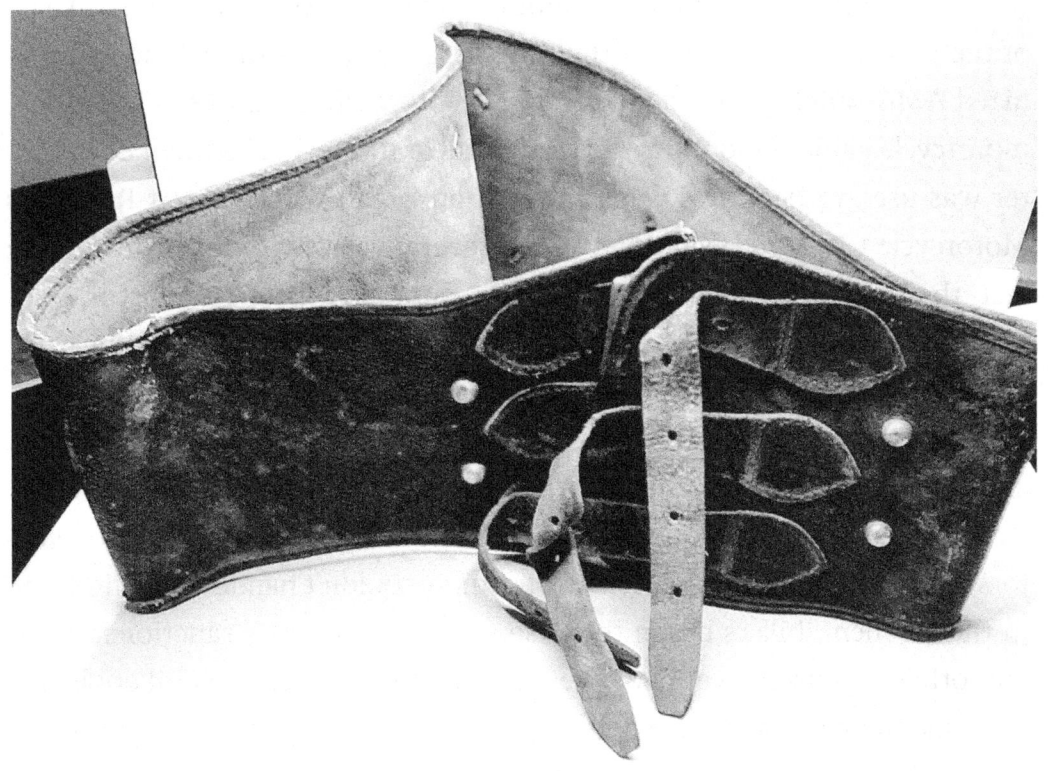

Kidney belt worn by Clarence Bendlin

PUBLIC OPINION AND THE HOLLISTER RIOT OF 1947

Up until 1947, the public was accepting of motorcycles and club members, even to the point of being enamored. That was all about to change. In just one event, not associated at all with members of the Ghost Chasers, the entire public outlook towards motorcycling culture changed for the next several decades almost overnight. It was called the Hollister Riot and it was an event that changed the history of motorcycles and the public attitude toward motorcycle clubs.

In a tiny town in Northern California, a group of motorcyclists converged for a Gypsy Tour on the July fourth weekend in 1947. The site of the tour was Hollister, a small farming community of only 4500 people. Just like all of the popular Gypsy Tours of the time, this event was to include an organized AMA-sanctioned dirt track race, a motorcycle scramble, a hill climb, motorcycle games, and tours of area points of interest. The town of Hollister was used to hosting a Gypsy Tour sponsored by the Salinas Ramblers Motorcycle Club, and had done so for several years without problems. In fact, the local businesses welcomed this event as it meant a boost in sales for the restaurants, motels, grocery stores, service stations, and taverns. However, the 1947 event was not at all what they were expecting.

Motorcyclists arrived in droves. They came from as far away as Connecticut and Florida, with large groups arriving from Los Angeles and San Francisco. By the end of the first day, townspeople were overwhelmed as over 4000 visitors arrived for the weekend. The town simply couldn't handle the influx, and in the mayhem, bikers began to cause trouble. The AMA-sanctioned races and other organized events of the weekend were ignored as bikers began to drink and party and raise hell. They drove their motorcycles right up to the bars in local taverns, they raced up and down the main street—ignoring the stoplights. They slept in the streets after finding all the motels or hotels had been overbooked. They overwhelmed the local hospital and it became jammed with injuries all the way into the parking lot. The poor police—just seven officers—tried to ticket those who were displaying disorderly conduct, public intoxication, reckless driving, etc. They even opened the courthouse for an evening session of night court to deal with the many infractions given. It was to no avail. Mayhem had arrived and the only thing that would bring quiet was for an end to the weekend, and a return to normalcy. Even the newspaper in faraway Winona, Minnesota, ran an article reporting that the police chief of Hollister had said, "If we'd have jailed everyone who deserved it, we'd have herded them in by the hundreds!"

The California Highway Patrol was called in and threatened the use of tear gas before the motorcyclists finally dispersed. By Sunday the media had gotten ahold of the story and it made headlines across the country—even earning a spread in *Life Magazine*. Dubbed the Hollister Riot, newspapers across the country and even Canada ran articles: "36 Hours of Turmoil: Stunting Motorcycles Run Riot in Streets" said the Calgary Herald on July 7, 1947. "Streets of California Town Scene of Bedlam" was the story run by the *Corpus Christi Times* in Texas.

The AMA was now in a PR nightmare. The general public became frightened that any minute their own town might be descended upon like the town of Hollister, with ruthless motorcycle hoodlums arriving in the nighttime and wreaking havoc. Many towns across the country went on to cancel scheduled motorcycle events. The AMA acted quickly, putting out a statement which said to the public that 99% of the motorcyclists are decent and law-abiding, and that only 1% had tarnished the reputation of the majority with their deviant behavior. The AMA also went on to discourage the wearing of military jackets with club insignia or riding "chopped" motorcycles. The AMA banned riders who did so from attending future AMA-sanctioned events. Thus began the formation of Outlaw Motorcycle Gangs such as the Hell's Angels.

The events in Hollister got the attention of Hollywood, and the 1953 movie "The Wild One" was released with Marlon Brando playing the part of a rebellious motorcycle gang leader. He even rode his own personal motor-cycle, a Triumph, in the film. It was a controversial yet popular movie and is considered to be the original outlaw biker film. The movie was based in part on the Hollister Riots, but uses a storyline where two rival motorcycle gangs terrorize a small town after one of their leaders is thrown in jail. Many towns across the United States, and even in the United Kingdom, banned the movie from being shown due to concerns that it would incite juvenile delinquency and lack of respect for authority. For the most part, the public liked Marlon Brando, and the movie is recognized as having a significant influence on fashion and hairstyles of the time, albeit a negative effect on the public's view of groups of motorcycle riders.

The 1950s is now referred to as the Golden Age of Motorcycling, thanks to the quick action of the AMA and also movie star Marlon Brando. It is interesting to note that the town of Hollister went on to host their annual Gypsy Tour every 4th of July, and still does so today.

AMA patch worn on jacket or shirt

Both the riot in Hollister and the movie had some impact on the Ghost Chasers Club in Spencer, Iowa. Public opinion was important to the members of the Ghost Chasers, and they wanted to make it clear they were not asso-ciated with any antics such as the ones displayed. At the same time, many members of the Ghost Chasers dressed exactly as Marlon Brando dressed in this movie. They wore official Harley Davidson black leather motorcycle jackets, tall black leather engineer boots, and the same billed caps.

The Ghost Chasers worked to become an accepted club in Spencer, Iowa. We can't be sure of the reason for the slowdown of their activities in Spencer around this time period, but a pattern can be seen for moving hill climbs and other races to neighboring small towns.

The official Ghost Chasers Club Motorcycle Jacket "colors." This patch is bright green with gold embroidery. Insignia like this served as a visual shorthand to convey the rider's affiliation and achievements. (Clarence Bendlin collection)

Harley Davidson Motorcycle Jacket insignia patch (Clarence Bendlin collection)

*Harley Davidson motorcycle cap worn by Clarence Bendlin with Gypsy Tour 1948 pin and
10 years of AMA Motorcycle pins, including diamond "veteran" 10-year pin in center.*

SIOUX RAPIDS HILL CLIMBS 1946-1952

Hill Climb 1946 at new location in Sioux Rapids

The Ghost Chasers continued to sponsor an annual hill climb after they reorganized following World War II. Guy Huginon's farm near Spencer, where the first three hill climbs were held, had become the location of a new dirt obstacle track where the club now sponsored TT races.

The Ghost Chasers moved their fourth hill climb to Sioux Rapids and sponsored a hill climb there on Sunday, September 29, 1946. From this point forward, for several years, Sioux Rapids would be the site of the hill climbs. An article in the *Sioux Rapids Bulletin Press* gave directions to get to the new location: "1½ miles east of town at the Oak Logvillion." Ghost Chasers founder Bob Wright serves as the referee at this climb and thirty riders were expected to enter. "45 and 80 cubic inch machines will compete in each event. The first event will be bare tire riding, each class. Chain riding, each class, and the final event will be open" ["Ghost Chasers Motorcycle Club to Hold Hill Climb," 1946, p. 1]. The club awarded cash prizes to the winners.

The hill chosen for the event was described as "clay bank and 90 feet tall with a 75% grade" ["Fans Thrilled by Hill Climb," 1946, p. 2]. There were only 15 competitors that day, but the crowd was treated to many chills and spills. Local favorite Jess Young entered the 80 cubic inch class and ended up roaring over the top of the hill in 6.2 seconds, winning first place in that event. Another club member, Bob Felton, on a light 45, went over the top in 4.2 seconds to win the final open event.

Ghost Chasers Motorcycle Club member Charlie Gilmore shared that the Oak Logvillion was a popular meeting space and ballroom similar to the Woodcliff Ballroom outside of Spencer. His mother had won a newspaper contest to name it and had picked Oak Logvillion due to the large number of oak trees around it and because it was going to be used in a similar way to other local dance halls of the day, often referred to as pavilions.

The hill that they climbed in Sioux Rapids (Photo courtesy of Singelstad Family, S. Morton, Tator Gilmore, G. White

Line-up of motorcycles at hill climb. Mary Jane Bendlin, then unidentified riders

Mary Jane Bendlin, line-up of motorcycles at hill climb

The Oak Logvillion had a stage and dance floor for traveling bands such as Lawrence Welk's, as well as local bands like Ghost Chaser member Ralph Easton and his Orchestra, who played there at least once, on July 12, 1947, for a Sioux Rapids American Legion and Lions Club dance. There was also a bar where drinks could be ordered. The hill for the Ghost Chasers hill climb was made easy to find by giving the Oak Logvillion as the landmark. Signs would then direct people to the hill climb area.

Sioux Rapids Hill Climb 1947

The second annual Sioux Rapids hill climb was once again held near the Oak Logvillion on Sunday, July 6. This was the fifth hill climb sponsored by the Ghost Chasers, and the second time it was held in Sioux Rapids. An estimated 500 spectators came to watch. The winners included two Ghost Chasers members. In the 45 Bare Tire event, third place went to Jess Young. In the 80 Bare Tire event, Bob Booth won third place. The 45 Chain event listed Jess Young as 2nd. In the 80 Chain event, Bob Booth was 2nd, as well as taking 3rd in the 80 Open event. The reporter covering the race said, "I don't believe anyone was disappointed. There were plenty of thrills and a few spills, and an excellent exhibition of good riding and showmanship" ["Hill Climb Held in Sioux Rapids Sunday," 1947, p. 1].

GHOST CHASERS MEMBERS HAVE CLOSE CALLS

It took five and a half weeks in the Saint Joseph Hospital in Sioux City before Ghost Chasers member Kenney Mansfield was cleared to return home. The accident had happened on a Saturday evening, August 2, 1947, while hill climbing east of Sioux Rapids. His machine went out of gear and started down the hill backward. Kenneth jumped to get out of the way, but was caught. A gash three inches deep was cut in the fleshy part of his leg above the knee. The gash was closed up with 18 stitches, but he was said to be bedridden in considerable pain.

Eleven days later, on the evening of August 13, Kenney was transported to the hospital in serious condition, reportedly from the motorcycle accident he experienced earlier that month ["Ken Mansfield in St. Joseph Hospital," 14 August, 1947, p. 1]. The next report in the *Sioux Rapids Bulletin Press* told that he was sent home from the Sioux City hospital after a lengthy stay. No doubt a serious infection had set in to the injured leg ["Ken Mansfield Injured in Motorcycle Accident," 1947, p. 1].

That same week, on August 6, 1947, a group of motorcyclists were climbing a hill in the gulch north of town. Ghost Chasers member "Art Rhodes' machine went down the hill backward, but he was able to jump free of it. When he started up the hill again, the machine burst into flames, caused no doubt by gasoline spilled on it in the accident" ["Ken Mansfield Injured," 1947, p. 1]. The fire department was called, but the flames were extinguished before they arrived. No injuries were reported.

This was not the first time Ghost Chasers member Kenny Mansfield had a close call on a motorcycle. While trying out a new motorcycle on the morning of Monday, June 10, 1946, Kenny was driving on Highway 71 when he hit the crossing tracks and went for a spill. The machine developed a high-speed wobble and left the highway. Kenny was unable to ride it down, so he rolled off the bike backwards. The bike traveled several yards without him, struck a tree, caromed thirty feet, and caught fire. Needless to say, the bike was a total loss. Kenny walked away with scratched elbows ["Kenny Mansfield In Motorcycle Spill," 1946, p. 1].

MEMORIES OF HILL CLIMBS IN SIOUX RAPIDS

Bob Bendlin remembers, "Our dad, Clarence, went everywhere on his bike (this was a 1947 Harley Davidson Knucklehead), and mom often rode along." Bob recalls that "when they wanted to go to a hill climb in Sioux Rapids, dad would start the bike and younger brother Larry (age 2 or 3) would get hoisted up in front of dad to ride on the gas tank, I (two years older) would get helped on behind dad, and then Mom would hop on behind the three of us, and off we'd go. All four of us would ride on that motorcycle in this way, over to our grandparents' farm—a distance of about 3 miles on gravel roads.

Once at our grandparents', Larry (the youngest) would be left and then Dad, Mom, and I would all ride on the motorcycle over to Sioux Rapids to the hill climb. From the Bendlin farm to the hill climb events in Sioux Rapids was a distance of about 20 miles. And then we'd ride home again at the end of the day the same way.

"These hill climbs were held along the bluffs over the river in Sioux Rapids. The racers who went up the hills were using stripped-down bikes with no windshields and no fenders. The motorcycles made ruts after the first few riders went up the designated hill. There would be guys measuring the distance the competitor got up the hill and they would see who went the farthest."

We know from their stories that dad was typically involved in the jobs of helping to manage the climb as a member of the Ghost Chasers. We see him in his pith helmet, along with several other members, manning the lines and helping to catch bikes that might injure spectators. Our mom was often the one on the sidelines using the movie camera to record the climbs. There are pictures of row upon row of bikes parked out in a field with some of the women sitting and waiting. Waiting for the hill climb to start? Waiting when the hill climb was over for the club members to take down the course?

Sioux Rapids Hill Climb 1948

The third hill climb in Sioux Rapids (the sixth one sponsored by the Ghost Chasers Motorcycle Club) was held once again at a hill near the Oak Logvillion. From an advertisement found on page 4 of the *Sioux Rapids Bulletin Press*, readers are advised of a "New and Better Hill 2½ miles East of where Hiway 10 turns West." The event was held on Sunday, July 25, at 2:00 p.m. Admission was raised to $1.00 and parking was free. The hill climb was AMA-sanctioned and sponsored by the Ghost Chasers Motorcycle Club ["Motorcycle Hill Climb," 1948, p. 4].

A newspaper article in the *Sioux Rapids Bulletin Press* reported that the Ghost Chasers Motorcycle Club believes they have found the ideal location. The directions to the new location are given in the article: "2½ miles east of where Highway 10 turns west." The only local entrant to the event was local favorite Jess Young from Sioux Rapids. There was going to be $350.00 for prize money, divided up in this manner: 45% for expert class awards, 35% to the amateurs, and 25% to the novices. For the convenience of the public, a soft drink stand will be available ["Motorcycle Hill Climb Here Sunday," 1948, p. 1].

Sioux Rapids Hill Climb 1949

The Ghost Chasers announced their fourth annual hill climb in the *Sioux Rapids Bulletin Press*. "Large purses and the love of excitement promise to draw cyclists from far distant points" ["Cycle Event Here Sunday, July 10," 7 July, 1949, p. 1]. The climb was held on the same hill as the one used the year before, near the Oak Logvillion. The entries included hometown favorite Jess Young, who was referred to as the town marshal. An ad was also placed by the Ghost Chasers and appeared in the same issue of the *Sioux Rapids Bulletin Press* on page 5. The admission charge for spectators was $1.00, children under 12 free. The climb would start at 2:00 and promised thrills and spills.

The Sioux Rapids Bulletin Press reported the results of the hill climb on the front page. Jess Young had taken second place in the Novice "45" class. There were around 35 cyclists entered, and a large crowd had attended. The rules for the hill climb were explained: "Each rider could drive two models, '45' and '30.' Each rider got two tries to climb the hill. Awards were made by footage climbed and time" ["Young Second in Hill Climb Here," 14 July, 1949, p. 1.].

Sioux Rapids Hill Climbs 1950

Hill climbs had become so successful that the Ghost Chasers decided to sponsor not one, but two climbs during the 1950 season. At an early spring dinner meeting on March 2, 1950, Jess Young told the reporter for the *Sioux Rapids Bulletin Press* that a delegation from the club would travel to Des Moines in the near future to coordinate dates for the two AMA-sanctioned events. At this same meeting motorcycle dealers from Sioux Falls came to present filmstrips of the Sioux Rapids hill climb from the previous fall as well as films of the 1949 Clay County Fairgrounds race. The location of the meeting was at the schoolhouse located three-fourths mile west of the Royal corner on Highway 71 ["Two Hill Climbs Here This Season," 1950, p. 1].

The Ghost Chasers held their fifth Sioux Rapids hill climb on Sunday, May 7, at 2:00 p.m. The event was near the Oak Logvillion and was an AMA-sanctioned one-star event ["Motorcycle Hill Climb Sunday," 1950, p. 1]. A huge crowd of 1500 spectators watched this hill climb and the 40 drivers who competed. "A woman spectator received leg cuts when one of the motorcycles veered into the crowd near the top of the hill" ["Large Crowd Views Motorcycle Event," 1950. P. 1]. Ghost Chasers member and local favorite Jess Young did compete but was not listed as a winner. One winner in the novice division, Bob Pieper of Waterloo, had the fastest climb at 3:06 seconds. This was "only a fraction of a second off the national record on a 100-foot hill."

The second hill climb of 1950 (the sixth one in Sioux Rapids) was held on Sunday, July 23rd. An "outstanding crowd" witnessed this hill climb, sponsored by the Ghost Chasers ["Hill Climb Big Success Sunday," 1950, p. 1]. One cycle had gone on a rampage, causing the crowd to quickly disperse, but the rider ended up catching his bike and only breaking his glasses. The report said that the riders were to start from a stopped position and then see how quickly they can climb the steep hill, if possible. Jess Young won both the amateur and the novice divisions.

The Ghost Chasers held a third, more somber hill climb near the Oak Logvillion in 1950, and one they had not planned to host. A benefit hill climb, with all proceeds and prize money to be donated to former member Jess Young, the hometown favorite, was held on September 3.

Jess Young had apparently stopped his membership in the club and was solely focused on his racing and hill climbing circuit by the late summer of 1950. His luck ran out while racing on the track in Blue Earth, Minnesota. He broke his back and was taken to the hospital in Sioux City, but was recovering enough to be expected home to recuperate. In order to lend support and help pay hospital bills, the Ghost Chasers stepped in to help ["Benefit Hill Climb For Jess Young," 1950, p. 1].

The hill climb was well attended, and the community stepped up, with a "liberal amount given by spectators and riders alike to a fund for Jess Young" ["Large Crowd at Benefit Hill Climb," 1950, p. 1]. The article in the Sioux Rapids Bulletin Press goes on to tell that Jess Young had arrived home Friday night from the Sioux City hospital. "The Young home was full of well-wishers and friends from early morning until late at night Sunday." The Youngs expressed gratitude for their help. Jess Young would remain bedridden for six weeks.

Sioux Rapids Hill Climb 1951

A newspaper advertisement from the *Sioux Rapids Bulletin Press* June 28, 1951, shows evidence of the 1951 hill climb held at the Oak Logvillion and sponsored by the Ghost Chasers. This is the seventh hill climb in Sioux Rapids. The date of this climb was Sunday, July 1, and is advertised as an AMA-sanctioned event. An article in the same newspaper informed the public that this will be the first hill climb of the season. "The sport event will take place at 2 o'clock at the Oak Logvillion hill located just east of Sioux Rapids" ["Motorcycle Climb Sunday," July 1st, 1951, p. 1]. There is no mention of local favorite Jess Young.

Sioux Rapids Hill Climb 1952

The Ghost Chasers continue their crowd-pleasing hill climb events in Sioux Rapids by hosting one on Sunday, July 20. It was the first climb of the season, AMA-sanctioned, and at a new location. From a newspaper article in the *Sioux Rapids Bulletin Press*, "The new hill is located North of Sioux Rapids and signs will be erected from the bridge on Highway 71 to the site of the new event" ["Motorcycle Hill Climb Sunday," 1952, p. 1].

An advertisement from the *Sioux Rapids Bulletin Press* confirms the new hill location, "Follow the Arrows Starting at the Bridge on Hi-way 71 to the Site. Longer Hill—More Spills" ["Motorcycle Hill Climb," 1952, p. 6]. "Jess Young, who will participate Sunday, stated that the new hill is longer and will offer more thrills for the crowd than the previous location." Young, the hometown favorite, was back in the action. He attended a race in Canton, South Dakota the previous weekend and placed fourth.

Even the *Spencer Daily Reporter* covered this hill climb in an article on July 21, 1952. The hill was described as 150 feet with a 60-degree angle. In the 45-inch expert class, Jesse Young of Sioux Rapids placed second. Dean Kelcey of Iowa Falls beat him with a climb of 7.8 seconds. The fastest time in the hill climb was Jim Kearney of Waterloo, with a time of 4.8 seconds in the 74-cubic inch expert class ["Jim Kearney Climbs Hill In 4.8 Time," 1952, p.?].

The *Sioux Rapids Bulletin Press* reported that Jesse Young won twice, capturing two second place finishes in the 45-inch expert class and in the 45-inch novice class ["Jess Young Wins Twice at Hill Climb," 1952, p. 8].

THE OKOBOJI SPEED BOWL 1952-1955

The Okoboji Speed Bowl, located on Highway 71 just north of Milford, opened in June 1952. The first season of their opening they held stock car races and midget car races nearly every weekend. It wasn't until the following Memorial Day in 1953 that the Ghost Chasers Motorcycle Club became involved in sponsoring and managing motorcycle races there as well. The motorcycle races preceded the stock car races and were very popular.

The Speed Bowl was the brainchild of local man, Jim Travis, who owned the Strand Theater in downtown Milford, as well as the Lakeland Drive-In Theater, which had opened in 1948 and operated until 1991. He was well known as a local theater "wheel" who rubbed shoulders with the likes of Ronald Reagan at a National Theater Convention in Omaha, and loved not only theaters, but auto racing.

He and his hired manager, Jack Paul of nearby Lake Park, devised a plan to invest $30,000 (equal to around $350,000 today) into extensive dirt moving near the site of the Lakeland Drive-In Theater, which was surrounded by 22 acres of unused land. Jack Paul was also a business partner who, along with Travis, had purchased the Sioux Speed Bowl in Cherokee as part of their race car and entertainment enterprise.

Their plan was to build the fastest third-mile track in the Midwest. This oval track was specially constructed for excessive speeds, with high banked curves at a four-to-one rise. Named a "Speed Bowl" because the track was dug out into a bowl shape, protective steel cable fences surrounded the entire track to protect spectators, and a double fence was constructed in front of the grandstand as an added safeguard. This grandstand was mounded up at the southeast corner of the property and held 3000 seats. Before it was finished, workers at the site had moved 35,000–40,000 cubic yards of dirt.

The Speed Bowl opened for its first races on June 8, 1952. These were stock car races, and the track did not disappoint. It allowed for terrific speed for dirt tracks—averaging 90 m.p.h. for one lap. Travis and Paul continued their improvements of the Speed Bowl and by July had added floodlights all around the track for night racing. Further improvements were completed in 1955 when a new 5th mile track was built inside the original track to accommodate smaller type stock cars.

The Okoboji Speed Bowl opened for its second season on June 3 in 1954. It was announced in the *Milford Mail* that a special attraction would take place Sunday night, Memorial Day, May 30, when the Ghost Chasers Motorcycle Club of Spencer would sponsor an American motorcycle race. There would be "machines and drivers from several Midwest states, as well as hundreds of motorcycle riders from a 500-mile radius" ["Okoboji Speed Bowl Races to Open on Thursday," 3 June, 1954, p. 1]. These races were AMA-sanctioned one-star short track races.

Riders from South Dakota, New York, Minnesota, and Iowa came to race. The six fastest riders included local rider Ernie Singelstad of Spencer ["Four Wins Scored by Rider in Cycle Races," 1954, p. ?]. The Ghost Chasers Motorcycle Club sponsored and managed many motorcycle events at this location from 1953 until the Speed Bowl closed in 1958.

There is a sad note to the comings and goings at the Okoboji Speed Bowl. On February 15, 1957, manager Jack Paul had moved on to accept a position as a technical representative for Beech Aircraft Corporation in Wichita, Kansas. On April 4, 1958, he was on a job to deliver a special-built photographic airplane from Wichita to Ceylon for the government of Ceylon, which had purchased the plane. Paul had planned to stay 90 days in Ceylon before returning via commercial airline on an around-the-world trip over the Pacific Ocean. The trip was cut short when, fifteen miles from Naples in a heavy rainstorm, the Beech plane crashed in the Camaldoli Mountains, killing Paul and two other Wichita residents making the trip with him. He was just 31 years old.

Parking area at Okoboji Speed Bowl before races start
(Photo courtesy of Singelstad Family, T. Gilmore, S. Morton, G. White)

Today the Okoboji Speed Bowl is not recognizable. The bowl shape no longer exists at the site and one can find any remnants of the stadium. Today it is the Okoboji Village manufactured home community; prior to that it was farm ground. As a landmark, many people will remember that Old Tony's Drive In was right in front of the Lakeland Drive-In Theater and featured some of the area's first Italian food—their pizza and stromboli sandwiches were popular. Old Tony's, operated by Tony and Almeda Capiano of Des Moines, opened their eight-sided fast-food restaurant in 1955 and sold it to Jim Travis in 1966.

GYPSY TOURS

An interesting advertisement promoting the term "Gypsy Tour" was published in the *Evening News Republican* in Marshalltown, Iowa, on April 19, 1918. Jim Johnson, the local Harley Davidson distributor, promoted the idea of joining a motorcycle touring group: "The Gypsy Tours are coming! Going along? Be a gypsy for a couple of days. Swing into your saddle—take your sidecar pal. Join the motorcycle Gypsies with a new Harley Davidson. Ride in the 1918 National Gypsy Tours, June 15th and 16th. The 1917 Gypsy Tours were an unqualified success. The riders voted for them to be an annual festivity among motorcyclists" ["Gypsy Tours," 1918, p. 7.].

Gypsy Tours were AMA-sanctioned events that were held on a single weekend throughout the country. These Gypsy Tours had started in New Hampshire in 1917, and continue today.

In the year 1925 there were 212 Gypsy tours in the United States. The tours were suspended during World War II, but started up again in 1946.

The Gypsy Tours were usually overnight events and were typically organized by local motorcycle clubs. The tours started with an organized road ride to a favorite destination, and ended up at a park where games and competitions would be held. The organized rides were usually about 75 miles long, but sometimes shorter or much longer. Gypsy Tours were considered one of the best ways that motorcycle riders could all get together for a weekend of fun activities.

A glimpse into the fun activities held on a typical Gypsy Tour can be found in a program from a Black Hills Gypsy Tour held August 8, 9, and 10 in 1947 near Rapid City, South Dakota. It is highly likely that a few members of the Ghost Chasers Motorcycle Club were there. The program states that the first day would be spent riding through the unique scenery of the Black Hills area. The evening get-together would feature a supper served from a real old-fashioned chuck wagon. The evening would end with "interviews, singing, and other entertainment." It was typical for the Gypsy Tour events to include an evening dance to a live band or records, or it might be a field meet under lights with plenty of trophies for the winners.

A newspaper article in the *Rapid City Journal* on August 12, 1948, told of Gypsy Tour participants carrying tools with them in order to constantly tighten their motorcycle's bolts loosened by vibration, and to repair broken chains. The article goes on to tell of an expected 400 motorcyclists—most from out of state. Sunday's finale would be a "flaming board wall crash" as an added feature.

Visitors would have their choice of four different tour destinations all around the Black Hills. In the collection from Ghost Chasers Motorcycle Club member Clarence Bendlin, there is a Gypsy Tour buckle from the year 1948. The family believes it is from the Gypsy Tour held in Sturgis that year. Clarence and his wife Mary Jane enjoyed many trips to the Black Hills area during their early married years and often told stories of their participation in Gypsy Tours.

A newspaper article in the *Rapid City Journal* from August 12, 1949, reported that 500 motorcyclists attended the Gypsy Tour in Sturgis that summer. Bob Wright, charter member of the Ghost Chasers Motorcycle Club from Spencer, was the starter for the races. Miss Daisy Rundle of Monticello, Iowa, was named the Gypsy Queen from a field of nine contestants.

A 1949 account of the Gypsy Tour at Sturgis describes the activities at a meet. After arriving at the rally spot, there would be club parades where each club's riders would enter a centrally designated arena holding their club flags or banners. There they would line up for the uniformed club contest. There would be awards given for the "neatest appearing rider" and the one with the "cleanest motor." The types of awards given varied each year.

Activities held at a Gypsy Tour event were often races, including half-mile races, hill climbs, dirt track events, and field meets where motorcycle games were played and trophies and awards given.

Women were included in many of the games and contests. One award that was advertised for the 1949 Gypsy Tour was described as a "striking tie clasp with a small motorcycle attached" and an award for the ladies was a "charm bracelet with a miniature motorcycle dangling on a chain." In Ghost Chasers club member Clarence Bendlin's collection, there is a tie clasp with a small motorcycle attached, just as the one described in the program. We believe he won this at a contest while attending a Gypsy Tour.

Clarence Bendlin rode his Harley Davidson on several Gypsy Tours with other groups of riders, many of them members of the Ghost Chasers Motorcycle Club. Quite often these trips included the wives riding along as well. We know he went on a Gypsy Tour in 1948—no doubt in Sturgis—another Gypsy Tour in 1953 held north of Milford (at the Okoboji Speed Bow), and another one in 1955—also held at the Okoboji Speed Bowl. He kept souvenirs from these various Gypsy Tours—belt buckles, pins for his hat, and tie clips. In his collection, we found one dated 1948, one dated 1953, and three are dated 1955.

Motorcycle games were always a fun part of each Gypsy Tour. Harley Davidson published a "Booklet of Motorcycle Games" in 1950. It contained several pages of games to be played while riding a motorcycle.

A sampling of the games played at the Gypsy Tour events:

Whacking the Murphy: Each rider is armed with a broom handle or the like and tries to smash a large potato which is on top of a stake driven into the ground. The stake is planted vertically and is long enough to bring a potato to about the height of the rider's waist when mounted. Each rider takes a turn to ride his motorcycle at a minimum speed of 15 m.p.h. toward the stake and cut the potato downward in order to break the potato off the stake. Sidestrokes are not allowed.

Barrel Rolling: A starting line and a finish line are marked at least 50 feet apart. Two or more empty oil drums are laid out at the finish line on their sides. Contestants start the race with the front tire of their motorcycle against the oil drum. At the signal, the riders race to see who can roll their barrel across the finish line first. No one is allowed to touch the barrel with anything but the front tire of their bike.

Plank Race (minus plank): Two white strings are fastened on the ground about 10 inches apart for a distance of 50 feet. Contestants ride down between the strings as fast as they can go. All riders who stay between the strings advance to the next round. The strings are moved closer together, and the rounds continue until only one rider remains.

A variation of this game says players may be blindfolded to attempt to ride between the strings. They caution that with this variation the contest must allow only one rider at a time making the attempt.

Stake Race: Begin by driving 6 or more stakes into the ground, about 1 motorcycle length or more apart. All stakes should be driven vertically and protrude about 4 feet above the ground. Riders should start at one end, ride between the stakes to the opposite end, circle the last stake, and return by weaving between the stakes again back to the starting point. This is a timed event.

Quiz Run, or True and False Ride: Riders and their passengers may compete together. At the start, every rider is handed a slip of paper containing a question to be answered true or false. Example: "Registered riders rode an average of 300,347 miles per accident in 1950. If you believe this is true, ride to the intersection of Green Bay Road and Villard and find your next clue at the base of the telephone pole. If you believe this is false, go to the Blue Moon Inn and ask the cashier for your next clue." The game would proceed with as many other questions and locations as the organizers wished, but it always ended up back at the event site. The first motorcycle to get there would be the winner.

Other games listed included a side-car elimination race, an equilibrium race, and even a "grab the potato" race involving the couples who rode together. It was played like musical chairs, where all contestants rode their motorcycles in a large circle all at once, and on a given signal they stopped. The women on the back of the motorcycles had to jump off the bikes and race to a pile of potatoes located on the ground in the center of a large circle. They were to grab a potato to keep from being eliminated. There was always one less potato than riders, so the woman who ended up with no potato would get herself and her partner eliminated each time.

GYPSY TOURS AT THE OKOBOJI SPEED BOWL

*This was taken at the Gypsy Tour located at the Okoboji Speed Bowl in 1955.
Front center is Ernie Singelstad. (Photo courtesy of Singelstad family)*

Jim Travis, owner of the Okoboji Speed Bowl, was a supporter of local motorcycle enthusiasts and a great promoter of events. In a news article in the *Spirit Lake Beacon* on May 7, 1953, he told the reporter that a feature of the coming summer events would be a Gypsy Tour where Travis estimated 1000 motorcycles will come ["Motorcycle Races on Bowl Program," 1953, p. 8]. By July 30, the *Milford Mail* reported that 2000 motorcyclists were going to attend the AMA-sanctioned riding exhibition and racing event ["2000 Motorcyclists To Be In Territory Over This Weekend," 1953, p. 1].

The Gypsy Tour at the Speed Bowl was advertised far and wide. A "Want Ad" from the *Cedar Rapids Gazette* July 29, 1953, proclaimed: "Motorcyclists plan to attend the Iowa Gypsy Tour August 1 and 2 in Arnolds Park, Iowa. Two days of fun for everyone."

From the *Spirit Lake Beacon,* a rundown of the weekend's events on August 1 and 2 were listed, along with reassurance to the locals that a maximum of 800 cyclists (not 2000) would be in the area for the Gypsy Tour: "Field registration and meeting is scheduled for 2 o'clock Saturday afternoon at the Speed Bowl. That evening the motorcycles will be awarded trophies at the track, with activities (which included a full racing program) beginning at 8:00 p.m. Sunday morning the parade of motorcycles will tour through the entire Lakes region. The cyclists will split up in three groups and visit each of the Lakes towns. Sunday afternoon will be the short track races at the Okoboji Speed Bowl" ["Motorcycle Parade to Tour Lakes Area," 1953, p. 6].

The Gypsy Tour of 1953 appeared to come and go with little disruption to the local citizens throughout the lakes area. While no final attendance numbers could be found in local newspapers, it is believed that it was a highly successful gathering. We know that Ghost Chasers members were well represented at this event. One participant we have proof attended was Ghost Chasers member Clarence Bendlin. He kept a souvenir AMA license plate clip from this Gypsy Tour, dated 1953.

After the event, an interesting mention is made in a newspaper article on October 28, 1953. The *Sioux City Journal* published an article which told of a man named Elmer Burgess who was testifying in court about a murder that occurred at the Tangney Hotel in Spencer on August 1, 1953. His testimony states that he and his wife had stayed at the hotel because they had traveled on their motorcycles with other couples from Cedar Rapids—"about six of us"—to attend the Gypsy Tour in Milford. He further testified that the Gypsy Tour was "just North of here or Milford, there is a racetrack and outdoor theater" which was the location of the Gypsy Tour gathering. He had arrived in Spencer with his wife at about 9:00 in the evening. He said that he went to the Maid Rite and had supper. During the night, in a room opposite his room, he was awakened by an altercation. A murder was committed, which he had nothing to do with, but he was called as a witness who had heard the commotion ["Testimony Taken at Dillon Murder Trial," 1953, p. 14].

The Okoboji Speed Bowl hosted their second—and what was to be their last—Gypsy Tour in 1955. This Iowa Gypsy Tour motorcycle rally was held on August 6 and 7. It was planned to be very similar to the tour held in 1953, with registration at the bowl on Saturday morning followed by a field meet where motorcycle games would be played and trophies awarded. Saturday evening there would be a one-star Class C short track race. Then on Sunday morning, motorcyclists would make a tour around West Okoboji, stopping at Gull Point State Park for a picnic dinner (the noon meal). In the afternoon, riders would return to the Speed Bowl for the presentation of awards to motorcycle clubs, followed by another short track race on their larger track.

The Ghost Chasers Motorcycle Club participated in all the weekend's festivities. In the Clarence Bendlin collection, we have three Gypsy Tour belt buckles from this event. Further, the Ernie Singelstad family has shared for display at the Clay County Heritage Center a large panoramic framed photo that Ernie displayed in his shop until the shop closed, and then displayed in his home. Taken of participants at this Gypsy Tour, it shows a sizable group of motorcycle riders posing in rows. Ernie is shown in the front row, direct center.

The dust settled and quiet resumed after the more than 1000 motorcycles, carrying over 1200 individuals, roared for home late Sunday night and Monday. Local newspaper reports expressed some dismay at the antics of a few rogue visitors—especially those from Saint Paul, Minnesota. A report in the *Milford Mail* said that many in the community had mixed emotions about the influx of over 1000 motorcycles, primarily from Iowa and Minnesota. Most of the bikes contained only one rider, but some carried two, and quite a few carried a man, woman and child. These totaled more than 1200 people who quickly filled up all available rooms in the area. While they were well behaved for the most part, the large group held some rabble-rousers.

Considerable trouble was caused by the "complete unit" from St. Paul, Minnesota, with several of them ending up in area jails. According to reports from attendees, the St. Paul riders had previously been barred from any participation in Minnesota meets due to their untenable behavior. So, of course, since Iowa had not barred them, they assumed they would be welcome to attend the Gypsy Tour at the Okoboji Speed Bowl. "Several of the group were apprehended by law enforcement officers in both Arnolds Park and Spirit Lake. One group caused considerable trouble in a Milford tavern and had threatened to wreck the place."

1953 Gypsy Tour AMA license plate clip

Nan Ayres, from Minneapolis was lodged in the Milford jail on Sunday night, charged with operating a motor vehicle while intoxicated. Her ex-husband, William Hoese of St. Paul, was jailed in Spencer on a charge of refusing to assist an officer in an arrest. Both had come together to the Speed Bowl in a high-powered racing Ford and were apprehended there after being chased between Spencer and the lakes. Monday evening, Nan pled guilty before Judge H. E. Narey and paid her fine of $300 dollars and $31.00 court costs (equivalent to $3,500 today). She then drove to Spencer where she paid the fines and court costs of Mr. Hoese—a more reasonable $50.00 fine—so he could be released and travel with her on their exit from the area.

1955 Gypsy Tour Gold AMA belt buckle (Clarence Bendlin collection)

Gypsy Tour gold motorcycle tie clasp (Clarence Bendlin collection)

It was no wonder that many area citizens questioned whether the cyclists should be allowed to return. The article did say that two years prior, the group was very orderly and had enjoyed their visit to the lakes. However, one thing is sure: "Local law enforcement officials say that if they do return, they will be prosecuted for every violation of the law" ["More Than 1,000 Motorcycles in Area Over Weekend; Attend Gypsy Tour," 1955, p. 1]. What we know for certain is that this was the last Gypsy Tour held at the Okoboji Speed Bowl.

WALLINGFORD EVENTS

Wallingford, a small town just over 30 miles east and a bit north from Spencer, hosted motorcycle events from as early as 1940 ["Motorcycle Races," 24 October, 1940, p. 1]. The Ghost Chasers Motorcycle Club sponsored the Fourth of July motorcycle races there at the Wallingford Ball Park in 1954, which included a TT race over a specially designed course ["List Full Day's Program for Wallingford's Third Annual Big July Fourth Celebration," 1 July, 1954, p. 1]. There is an advertisement in the *Graettinger Times* for Wallingford's Annual 4th of July Celebration of 1956 with events listed. The Ghost Chasers Motorcycle Club is scheduled for 3:00 p.m. with motorcycle races and a TT Race. The notation says this is for club riders only. An article in the same issue says that the Ghost Chasers promise to provide thrills and top-notch competition ["Wallingford to Celebrate Fourth," 28 June, 1956, p. 1].

CLUB CONFLICT

Paul Currans said, "There were two motorcycle clubs in Northwest Iowa in the late 1940s and '50s. They were the Thunder Bolts in the Mallard area and the Ghost Chasers in the Spencer area. Sometime in the 1950s they merged to form the Ghost Chasers." This didn't work out and caused a division in the club from which it was difficult to recover. While the point of conflict is not spoken about today, it was a significant hurdle for the club to overcome.

Greg White shared an original ledger book which showed Ghost Chaser's club business from the year 1950 to 1957. Through these records, we can pinpoint the conflict and split must have occurred between 1950–1952. The club membership at that time had ballooned to 35 members. Nearly one half of the membership names have lines drawn through them in the ledger book. Two of the crossed-out names have a notation, "no dues paid," but the others give no explanation. Several of the crossed-out names are riders from Mallard and Ayrshire. The 1953 record book shows the club membership at just thirteen.

We can't know what the reason was for this downturn in membership, but at that time the typical life span of a motorcycle club was just three years. We do know that the Ghost Chasers Motorcycle Club was able to continue as a club and by 1957, membership was listed as 20 active members. With the wives, this would have been a large group of nearly 40 individuals.

The Ghost Chasers, like all the other motorcycle clubs, had members who might join only for one or two club-sponsored activities. They also had members who would stay for decades. Whatever the reasons for a member to depart from the club, it was often for obligations to growing families or, in some cases, the military.

GHOST CHASERS MOTORCYCLE CLUB 1950 MEMBERSHIP

From the collection of Greg White, a club ledger from 1950–1957 shows the following members. *Note:* Names are listed just as the ledger book shows them and may be misspelled.

1950–1951 Dues Paying Members

Duane Barglof (Greenville)

Ernie Singelstad (Spencer)

Bob Booth (Spencer)

*Robert Smith (Spencer/crossed out)

Leo Doyle (Ayrshire)

*Fred Sweet (Webb/crossed out)

Clarence Bendlin (Spencer)

Lowell Wade (Spencer)

Jack Boatman (Peterson)

Wendell Webster (Peterson)

*John Chapman (crossed out)

Vernie White (Mallard)

*LeRoy Dohlburg (Laurens/crossed out)

*Arnold White (Mallard/crossed out)

*Leo Doyle (Ayrshire/crossed out)

Bob Wright (Everly)

*John Hubling (Ayrshire/crossed out)

*LaVerne Ridenour (Mallard/crossed out)

John Ihry (Royal)

Jerry Lever (Mallard)

*Bill Koenig (Ayrshire/crossed out)

Vernard Barglof (Greenville)

Wayne Kress (Webb)

Kenneth Wolbur (Sheldon)

*Lowel Lewis (Sioux Rapids/crossed out)

Don Huisman (Fluisman?) (Sheldon)

*Kenny Mansfield (Sioux Rapids/crossed out)

*Richard VanRenner Jr. (Sheldon/crossed out)

*Dale (Bob?) Mohr (Spencer/crossed out)

*Jim Parks (Spencer/crossed out)

Darryl Miller (Spencer)

Albert Nessholfer (Mallard)

Roy Nielsen (Webb)

*Oscar Nordblad (Ruthven/crossed out)

Donald Peterson (Wallingford)

*Art Rhodes (Spencer/crossed out)

Ledger Book Member List February 3, 1953:

Clarence Bendlin (Spencer)

Roy Nielsen (Spencer

Ernie Singelstad (Spencer)

Lyall Beving (Spencer)

Johnny Giep (Spencer)

Marvin Jans (Fostoria)

Bob Hanson (Spencer)

Darrel Miller (Spenecer)

Lowell Wade (Spencer)

Kirby Anderson (Greenville)

Duane Barglof (Greenville)

Vernard Barglof (Greenville)

Bob Booth (Spencer)

The officers of 1953 are listed as follows:

President: Bob Hansen

Vice-President: Johnny Giep

Secretary: Roy R. Nielsen

In addition, there is a written page documenting some club minutes. It appears these minutes were taken at the meeting on February 3, 1953. The ledger reads, "Meetings to be 1st and 3rd Tuesday of every month. All agreed not to send cards out. Those present were Ernie Singelstad, Marvin Jans,

Johnny Giep, Vernard Barglof, Roy Nielsen, Bob Hansen, Duane Barglof, Lyle Beving. Voted on dues and agree to pay 50 cents per month, a total of $6.00 which is due before receiving membership cards. Started year with $510.85. Ended with $19.75."

Ghost Chasers Ledger Book Member List February, 1954

AMA 47184: Clarence Bendlin
AMA 57496: Jerry Capesius
AMA 83190: Roy Nielsen
AMA 57498: Philip Johnson (Rolfe)
AMA 78844: Howard Nielsen
AMA 33732: Dorothy Nielsen
AMA 30745: Ernie Singelstad
Richard Wills (Mallard)
AMA 71040: Albert Nesshoefer
*Dale Fink (Spencer/ crossed out)
*Lyle Beving (crossed out)
AMA 5352: Bill Bruger (Truesdale—incomplete AMA #)
*Johnny Giep (crossed out)
AMA 5332: Max Zinn (Storm Lake—incomplete AMA #)
AMA 85531: Marvin Jans
*George Weiland (Truesdale/crossed out/Army)
Bob Hanson (crossed out: notation "Army")
*Don Sievers (Storm Lake/crossed out)
AMA 80606: Vernard Barglof
Forrest Adams

It is of note that in this membership list from 1954 the first woman is listed with her own AMA number. This is Howard Nielsen's wife, Dorothy Nielsen. This shows that she no doubt operated her own motorcycle. Wives were considered to be members alongside their husbands, but were not counted in the attendance or business records of the club in the 1940s-1950s, and paid no dues.

The officers of 1954 are listed as follows:
  President: Howard Nielsen
  Vice-President: Marvin Jans
  Secretary: Albert Nesshoefer

In addition, the ledger book shows a written documentation of bank balances for the year 1954:

Bank balance 3/10:	**$48.79**
Bank Account:	**$167.09**
Wills, initiation, and dues:	+$11.00
Add club balance of	$42.79
	$209.88
Balance before paid:	**$59.79**
Whit(?)	-$35.00
Sanctions:	-$15.00
Balance:	**$174.88**
Club owes Ernie benevolence:	-$25.00
(?)	+$10.00
Balance after paid:	**$19.79**
Bank Account:	$184.88
Dues and initiation:	+$11.00
Dale Fink	-$30.79
AMA card, 902 East 8th	+$6.00
Balance:	**$36.79**
Vernard Barglof	+$6.00
Balance:	**$42.79**
Ending Account Balance:	**$27.66**

In the space between the bank account showing the ending balance of $27.66, there are subtractions showing $233.13 minus $44.80, leaving $188.33. Then on September 14, 1954, the balance shows $27.66. There must have been an event sponsored by the club that cost them around $160.00.

The Ghost Chasers held a mileage contest in 1954. Mileage contests were a popular activity with motorcycle clubs in the 1950s. Riders typically competed to achieve the highest fuel efficiency (miles per gallon) over a set amount of distance or time. The motorcycle's odometer was used to record a starting and ending number of miles ridden. The amount of fuel used was measured using a calibrated fuel gauge, or measuring the amount of fuel added to the tank. The mileage was then calculated by dividing the distance traveled by the amount of fuel used.

The rules of the Ghost Chasers mileage contest are not written, but the intent of many of their mileage contests was to ride a number of miles without any accident. The results from a 1954 was recorded:

Bill Brugger	10,631 *winner
Lyle Bevin	10,162
Marv Jans	14,577
Al Nesshoefer	12,580
Max Zinn	23,409
Roy Nielsen	5,758
Bob Hanson	22,895
George Werland	12,050
Gary Knudtson	23,700
Dick Wills	15,300

Ghost Chasers Ledger Book Member List January, 1955

AMA 47184: Clarence Bendlin

AMA 83190: Roy Nielsen

AMA 78844: Howard Nielsen

AMA 30745: Ernie Singelstad

AMA 85531: Marvin Jans

Vernard Barglof (Spencer/ crossed out)

AMA 71040: Albert Nesshoefer

AMA 5352: Bill Bruger (Truesdale)

Richard Wills (Mallard)

AMA 5332: Max Zinn (Storm Lake)

AMA 86397: Gary Knudtsen (Linn Grove)

Jerry Wills (Milford)

Don Sievers (Storm Lake/crossed out)

Milo Watson (Milford)

Don Peterson (Wallingford/crossed out)

Forest Adams (Spencer)

Oscor Nordblad (Ruthven)

The officers of 1955 are listed as follows:
   President: Howard Nielsen
   Vice-President: Clarence Bendlin
   Secretary/Treasurer: Marvin Jans

Ghost Chasers Ledger Book Member List January, 1956:

AMA 47184: Clarence Bendlin

AMA 83190: Roy Nielsen

AMA 78844: Howard Nielsen

AMA 30745: Ernie Singelstad

AMA 85531: Marvin Jans

AMA 71040: Albert Nesshoefer

AMA 58676: Richard Wills (Mallard)

AMA 5332: Max Zinn (Storm Lake)

AMA 86397: Gary Knudtsen (Linn Grove)

Jerry Wills (Milford)

Milo Watson (Milford)

George?

The officers of 1956 are listed as follows:
   President: Howard Nielsen
   Vice-President: Clarence Bendlin
   Secretary/Treasurer: Marvin Jans

Ghost Chasers Ledger Book Member List January, 1957

AMA 47184: Clarence Bendlin

AMA 83190: Roy Nielsen

AMA 78844: Howard Nielsen

AMA 30745: Ernie Singelstad

Forrest Adams

Oscar Nordblad

AMA 85531: Marvin Jans

AMA 71040: Albert Nesshoefer

AMA 58676: Richard Wills (Mallard)

AMA 5332: Max Zinn (Storm Lake/crossed out)

AMA 86397: Gary Knudtsen (Linn Grove/crossed out)

Greg White

Red Cox (crossed out)

Lowell Wade (Spencer)

Johnny Anderson

Jerry Wills (Milford)

Milo Watson (Milford)

Ralph Easton

The officers of 1957 are listed as follows:

   President: Richard Wills

   Vice-President: Ralph Easton & Sons

   Secretary: Marvin Jans

   Referee: Ernie Singelstad

Clarence Bendlin's AMA Card from 1957

The Ghost Chasers Motorcycle Club Membership 1960

Paul Currans (Ghost Chasers member from 1960s-1999) provided a list of Ghost Chasers Club Members he recalled from the early 1960s:

Paul Currans (Spencer)	Marvin Jans (Fostoria)
Jon Easton (Spencer)	Jerry Mills (Greenville)
Ralph Easton (Spencer)	Bob Napier (Webb)
Jerry Eischen (Spencer)	Gene Napier (Cornell)
Francis Ellis (Emmetsburg)	Albert Nesshoefer (Mallard)
Bob Grace (Mallard)	Rich Sorensen, (Spencer)
Dave Griffin (Ruthven)	Bob Studer (Rolph)
Dick Graham (Ruthven)	John Studer (Graettinger)
Art Hansen (Spencer)	Greg White (Spencer)
Mike Markley (Ruthven)	

Jerry Capesius *he went on to join JackPine Gysies

Greg White shared an original Ghost Chasers record book where attendance at club meetings and attendance at various club activities had been recorded.

From this book we learned which members listed "present" at meetings in 1968–1969. Membership in the Ghost Chasers changed each season as new people joined and some older members departed. This record shows that many new members have joined the club while only about half of the older members mentioned by Paul Currans are still in the club.

Paul Currans	V.E. "Gene" Napier
Sheila Currans	Dorothy Napier
Bill DePue	V. E. "Junior" Napier
Judy DePue	Judy Napier
Billy Eaton	Robert A. "Bobby" Napier
Frances Ellis	Albert Nesshoefer
Betty Ellis	Ann Nesshoefer
Russell "Dub" Gilbaugh	Ray Riecke
Charlie "Chuck" Gilmore	Helen Riecke
Dean Gilmore	Bob Sierck
Irene Gilmore	Delores Sierck
Art K. Hansen	Richard "Red" Sorensen
H. Maxine Hansen	Sue Sorensen
Marv Jans	John Studer
Norma Jans	Lois Studer
Mike Markley	Carmen Markley

When comparing the attendance records from the 1960s to the earlier 1950s, it is of note that the later attendance lists now recognize women in attendance. Paul Currans and his wife Sheila were longstanding members in the Ghost Chasers, starting in 1961 or 1962 and continuing until the Ghost Chasers club disbanded.

In an interview held October 2024, Paul Currans explained about membership in the 1960s, "The wives were considered members if they chose to be active. Many were active, some never.

"We had club meetings at a café in Graettinger quite a bit, but we met all over at several other cafes. When you joined the club, you got a membership card. Paid annual dues—$10.00 maybe. A new card was issued every year."

Paul Currans had the job of club secretary for a while, with the job to send cards for meetings. Other jobs of the secretary would be to sign off membership cards and keep track of attendance at meetings.

Sheila Currans used Artex Paints to decorate jackets for all the club members. At that time, the club members wore a bright blue nylon windbreaker jacket and the patch was white. She painted the patch with a ghost on a unicycle. Then she painted the name of the club across the patch. Each club member's name was also painted on the back of the jacket. Other than the windbreaker, most everyone wore boots when they rode, but typically they wore no uniform or anything else different from everyday clothes. She added that since everyone had kids, they were also careful when they rode.

*Greg and Pam White brought in one of these patches to the museum.

As far as the bikes the club members rode, Paul commented, "We rode all different kinds of motorcycles—British motorcycles, Harley Davidson, all kinds. I bought and sold… bought used Harleys, fixed them up. Traded, sold. I had a '61 Knucklehead I bought for $65.00. Had a '45 Harley—bought that in town. Had a Harley Sportster K model from Dick Winters in Langdon. It had lots of chrome. When I started—only Harleys and Indians were available used. A new Triumph was half the cost of a Harley."

NORTHWEST IOWA MOTORCYCLE EVENTS IN THE 1960S

Sioux Rapids 1962

The Ghost Chasers Motorcycle Club returned to Sioux Rapids to hold another hill climb on Sunday afternoon, June 17. The location was one mile east of Sioux Rapids, near the Oak Logvillion ["Cycle Hill Climb Sunday Afternoon," 14 June, 1962, p. 1].

Graettinger Events 1961–1971

Jeff Jans, son of Ghost Chasers member Marv Jans, recalled that there were Scramble Races held in Graettinger in the 1960s. Greg White, Ghost Chasers club member, noted that the Ghost Chasers Club also sponsored a hill climb every Labor Day for several years in Graettinger.

Ghost Chasers club member Paul Currans also shared memories about the Ghost Chasers club sponsoring hill climbs in Graettinger. He said, "The most successful one was south of Graettinger. We were 12 years or so at the same farm. It was Mae Zettrick's farm. We would advertise in a motorcycle newspaper or magazine—we could get people from all around. They came from Minneapolis, from Omaha, from Sioux Falls. There might be 100 or so riders. We split them up in classes based on engine size. One class for 125 or smaller, one for the 250s (that was the most popular class), another class for 500 (not many of those), and another class for 750 and bigger bikes. They were timed, and the one who got up the hill with the shortest time won. We gave out trophies."

Paul Currans continued, "There would be a list of riders and we'd call off the list and who was next. Most did not go all the way up—tipped over backwards sometimes. One guy from Sioux Falls came. His name was Danny Doobler. He was a National Rider. He went full throttle, started spinning.

He rode a Triumph 750. He came to every one of the area hill climbs that the Ghost Chasers sponsored. He was a fun character to watch, as he always would go full throttle and start spinning his tires, and every time he would be the winner. He rode a Triumph 750."

Paul also remembered, "Another guy was Albert Nesshofer. He was a Li'l Abner type. Looked like he came out of the field, in his coveralls and work boots. He didn't say much, but he'd come in and sign up and he always won."

Greg White recalled that Al Nesshoefer was from Mallard. "He came to the hill climbs wearing his bib overalls and farm boots, and the bottom of his bike would be just full of straw from running it through the fields. And he would win every damned time! He'd go right up over the top!" commented Greg.

Pam White agreed, saying, "He was quite a rider."

Greg remembered that one time, "Al won an enduro meet on a Cushman motor scooter. And he was racing against the big motorcycles!"

Charlie Gilmore also spoke about the Graettinger hill climbs. He was one of the boys who would be allowed by the older club members to have the job of parking cars. Then during the hill climb, he would be a "catcher" and run out on the track to try to corral the bikes that didn't make it to the top and were tumbling backwards down the hill. Laughing about it now, he recalled how dangerous that was and how there were really no safety measures or rules preventing the boys from doing this. They thought it was great fun, and it allowed them to be a part of the action.

Jeff Jans, son of Ghost Chasers member Marvin Jans, shared that one of the bikes his dad owned was a Maico. It was this Maico that he used to do hill climbs. He said, "Dad was out in Sturgis for Sturgis week out there. And they had a picture in a flyer showing him coming up off the hill and it said something like, 'you have to master your skills to even ride the hill climbs' and if you look real close at that picture, you can see the starting string straight across and he was already out of control before the clock started for him to go up!" Jeff also remembered his dad riding a BMW all the way out to the World's Fair in Seattle.

Many members of the Ghost Chasers Motorcycle Club live in and around the town of Graettinger, located approximately 30 miles east of Spencer. The first documentation that the Ghost Chasers Motorcycle Club had started to host motorcycle racing there was found in the *Graettinger Times* on May 4, 1961. The location of the event, held on May 7, was 2½ miles south of Graettinger, on the river road. This AMA-sanctioned event included field trial events for various classes of cycles and was open to the public.

On Sunday, July 2, 1961, the club held a hill climb near the same location, two miles south of Graettinger on the west side of the river ["Motorcycle Field Trials Here Sunday," 4 May, 1961, p. 1]. Spokesperson and president for the club, Russell Gilbaugh, referred to the club as the Northwest Iowa Ghost Chasers Motorcycle Club, and said the crowd was estimated at about 400. The hill proved to be tough competition for the thirty riders entered, who came from a wide area as far away as Sioux Falls and St. Paul. The event was declared most successful, with only one mishap: a Des Moines rider received a dislocated shoulder.

Local rider John Studer from Graettinger rode his Harley Davidson to a win in the 9 to 10 cu. inch category. Other locals placing were Albert Nesshoefer from Mallard, riding a Maico, and Bob Studer from Rolfe, riding a Maico. Other riders rode a variety of motorcycles which included Nortons, Triumphs, and Matchless bikes. The 110-foot hill was conquered by only one rider on a Harley Davidson, in 6.8 seconds. The rider, Irvin Andren from St. Paul, was entered in an open class ["Large Crowd at Cycle Hill Climb," 6 July, 1961, p. 1].

A Moto-Cross Scramble Race was sponsored by the Ghost Chasers Motorcycle Club in Graettinger on July 23, 1961. Club president Russell Gilbaugh explained the scoring system in an article in the *Graettinger Times*. "Riders were given points for each of three races, and the high-point rider was declared the winner of each classification. 400 points were awarded to the first-place rider in each race. 300 points were awarded for second, 225 for third, 169 for fourth, 127 for fifth place, and 9.5 for sixth. A score of 1200 points would mean the rider won all three races in his classification" ["List

Results of Recent Motorcycle Scramble Race Here," 3 August, 1961, p. 6]. Ghost Chasers Motorcycle Club members were highly successful at this race. In the 125 CC class, John Studer won with 1200 points, followed by Eugene Studer with 825 points. In the 200 CC class, Al Nesshoeffer won with 1200 points, followed by Marv Jans with 750 points.

News of a Ghost Chasers Motorcycle Club rally event appeared in the *Graettinger Times* in August 1961. The town's two-day Labor Day Celebration would include a hill climb sponsored by the Ghost Chasers on their club grounds southeast of Graettinger. The Ghost Chasers planned a camp out on Saturday evening following a road run. On Sunday morning, August 31, they would have a field meet at 9:00 a.m. and the hill climb at 1:00 ["Announce Labor Day Program for Two-Day Celebration," 21 August, 1961, p. 1].

The Ghost Chasers sponsored another very successful hill climb during the 1962 Labor Day Celebration in Graettinger, on Sunday, September 2. A few weeks later, on Sunday, October 14, the club sponsored an AMA motorcycle scramble race. The location in the newspaper was described as a mile south of Graettinger, then east on the river road ["Motorcycle Scramble Races Here Next Sunday Afternoon," 11 October, 1962, p. 1].

Motorcycle scramble races were held in Graettinger on Memorial Day, 1963. The location is referred to as the club grounds located on the river road, two miles south of Graettinger. "Club officials stated that an adequate public address system will be used so that spectators will be able to hear the race announcements" ["Motorcycle Scramble Races Slated Here on Memorial Day," 23 May, 1963, p. 1].

The club also returned to Graettinger's Three-Day Labor Day Celebration with a hill climb on Sunday afternoon, September 1st. "The club will repeat its program of last year, holding their 'Iowa Great Lakes Rally,' starting Saturday night with a rocket run and a field meet at 10:00 a.m. on Sunday" ["Motorcycle Rally Here This Weekend," 29 August 1963, p. 1]. The hill climb drew 28 entries and was watched by 425 citizens. John Studer, representing the Ghost Chasers, placed third in the 125-inch hill climb class and first in the 0-15 field event; Gene Studer was second in the same event ["Cycle Hill Climb Draws Large Crowd and Many Entries," 5 September, 1963, p. 1].

The 68th Annual Labor Day Celebration in Graettinger included a hill climb sponsored by the Ghost Chasers on their club grounds, south on river road. This hill climb was held on Sunday, September 6th ["7.6 Inches of Rain Here Labor Day, Flooding Follows," 10 September, 1964, p. 1].

The Annual Graettinger Labor Day celebration also included a Ghost Chaser's Motorcycle Club hill climb in 1965 and 1966. Results of the climb held in 1966 can be found in the *Graettinger Times*. Ghost Chasers Motorcycle Club members John Studer placed first in the 50 cc to 125 cc class, and Gene Studer came in second in the 175 cc to 200 cc class ["List Results of Cycle Hill Climb," 15 September, 1966, p. 1].

Graettinger's 71st Annual Labor Day Celebration was held on September 1 and 2, 1967. The Ghost Chasers Motorcycle Club participated with a rocket run on Saturday night, with a field meet and hill climb on Sunday. Results for the field events were posted and show a very imaginative mix of games. There was a String Ride, won by Ed Berchenbriter from Estherville; the Can Ride was won by Jr. Napier of Cornell; coming in first in the Wheelie Contest was Irlan Dalen from Estherville; the Tin Can Pick-Up was won by Ben Schoemaker of Sioux City; the Ladies' Race was won by Beth Anderson of Ft. Dodge; the Ladies' Boot Race was won by Mr. and Mrs. Doug Peterson of Linn Grove, and the Rocket Run was won by Roy Robinson of Des Moines ["Motorcycle Hill Climb Results Are Listed," 7 September, 1967, p. 1, p. 5].

The year 1968 held a first at the Ghost Chasers Annual Labor Day Hill Climb and Rally in Graettinger, on September 1st and 2nd. There was a Powder Puff Event, where hometown Graettinger rider Sue Studer, riding a Harley Davidson 125, grabbed the day's headline in the *Graettinger Times* by placing in the race against a field of riders from many other towns. Other field events were a Wheelie Contest, a Can Pickup, a Plank Race, and the popular Rocket Run ["Motorcycle Hill Climb Results; Sue Studer Places in Powder Puff Event," 19 September, 1968, p. 1, p. 6].

The Ghost Chasers followed suit in 1969, with their annual events to be held in conjunction with the town's 73rd Annual Labor Day Celebration. The Ghost Chasers started with a Road Run on Saturday evening, August 30, followed by a camp out. On Sunday morning, they held a field meet, and at 1:00 the crowds were treated to the hill climb event. The results of the hill climb showed Ghost Chasers Motorcycle Club members John Studer of Graettinger taking third place in the 0-125 class, and Richard Sorensen from Spencer placed third in the 201-250 class.

The Graettinger Labor Day celebrations included the Ghost Chasers Motorcycle Club sponsoring hill climbs into the 1970s, with newspaper documentation found for both 1970 and 1971. The hill climb event was always a crowd pleaser, with hundreds of motorcyclists converging on the Ghost Chasers Motorcycle Club riding grounds to watch the daring feats of the men who launched themselves upward to conquer the 110-foot-tall hill.

The winners line-up includes Marvin Jans, John Studer, Al Nesshoefer
(Photo courtesy of Tator Gilmore, Dean Gilmore collection)

Ghost Chasers members on a Poker Run
(Photo courtesy of Tator Gilmore, Dean Gilmore collection)

Ghost Chasers members in back: Marv Jans, John Studer, Al Nesshoefer
(Photo courtesy of Tator Gilmore, Dean Gilmore collection)

Hill Climb in Graettinger with Maico motorcycle
(Photo courtesy of Tator Gilmore, Dean Gilmore collection)

John Studer and Marvin Jans in Graettinger
(Photo courtesy of Tator Gilmore, Dean Gilmore collection)

The Graettinger Hill Climb, looking down the hill from top (Photo courtesy of Tator Gilmore, Dean Gilmore collection)

Graettinger Hill Climb, a rider mid-climb (Photo courtesy of Tator Gilmore, Dean Gilmore collection)

Graettinger Hill Climb, rider moving a cycle
(Photo courtesy of Tator Gilmore, Dean Gilmore collection)

TT Races in Graettinger
(Photo courtesy of Tator Gilmore, Dean Gilmore collection)

Graettinger TT Race Lap
(Photo courtesy of Tator Gilmore, Dean Gilmore collection)

Al Nesshoefer, cycle dealer in Mallard, towing cycles behind his 1954 Ford convertible
(Photo courtesy of Tator Gilmore, Dean Gilmore collection)

BSA Twin Cycle, Bob Studer on right
(Photo courtesy of Tator Gilmore, Dean Gilmore collection)

GOAT HILL

Image of Goat Hill today

Sitting high on a windswept hill above U.S. Highway 71, about 12 miles south of Spencer, stands an old landmark. Named "Goat Hill" by the locals, this tall and lonely home has stood uninhabited since the death of its one-time owner, Mr. Jess Ditton, in 1957. It is a strong house, built of concrete, kept company today by a field of wild meadow grasses and wildflowers. Jesse Ditton lived on this 140-acre farm his entire life.

His father, Mr. George Ditton, was a Civil War veteran who had arrived in Iowa and homesteaded that spot after the war ended. He and his wife Jestina lived first in a log cabin where Jesse was born on March 25, 1871. The concrete house was built at the same site over the course of a few years.

His parents were among those early settlers who told of fleeing to Fort Dodge for protection from the Indians after the Spirit Lake Massacre in 1857. His father died in 1872, when Jesse was just a year old. His mother stayed strong and managed the farm from then on. He did have siblings—a brother and a sister, both of whom grew up and moved on. Jesse and his mother remained there, and he farmed the land when he became old enough.

His mother passed away in 1901, and Jesse continued living alone. He was lonely, and would have liked a wife. The two he married ended up leaving him in rather short order due to his kindness toward his white goats. In the summer, the goats grazed on the hillside and drank from a trough to quench their thirst, but in the winter, he brought his goats inside the house to stay. Jess would often let some of the goats climb into the back seat of his Model T Ford as well to go for rides, and he said they seemed to enjoy it. The women who answered Jesse's want ads looking for a mail order bride or housekeeper or companion found the fact that his goats were inside the house untenable. One after another, they left. This only helped cement the local name for the house on the hill where the white goats grazed. It continues to be called Goat Hill to this day.

In 1940, when Jesse was 68 years old, an article and picture appeared in the Sioux City Journal. Jesse had become well known for his hobby of painting on the walls of his concrete home. In his spare time, he painted huge American flags on the outside walls. He liked the game of checkers, so he added red, white, and blue checkerboards in various places ["Jesse Ditton Standing Beside His Farm Home," *The Sioux City Journal*, 17 November, 1940, p. 12]. Later, Jesse allowed large painted advertising for the Clay County Fair to be painted on those walls, a sort of billboard advertising right up there on his house on the hill. He was always interested in the affairs of the community, and enjoyed attending carnivals and celebrations, and was fond of going to the fair.

Years after Jesse Ditton's death, Jeff Jans also remembered there was a Goat Hill scramble race held on Labor Day for several years. It was held on a dirt course circling around the house on Goat Hill.

Greg White remembered the Ghost Chasers Motorcycle Club sponsored races at Goat Hill outside of Spencer. "At the time I suppose we would have called it a motocross race or an enduro race, up and down the hill and around. And there was one young fellow in the morning that was testing his bike around there, and they wanted (him to clear the track) they kept waving him in, time to shut 'em off, you know, and he just wouldn't quit... he just wouldn't quit... and unfortunately—I think your dad told me this (Jeff's dad Marvin Jans)—they finally moved a late 40 combine crossways across the track and he ran right into it. So that was a bad deal. So that's about all I remember on that." The Ghost Chasers as a whole didn't have much patience for a rogue rider in their midst.

Bob Bendlin was also at one of the Goat Hill scramble races with his future wife, Sue. He had been given rare permission to ride Clarence Bendlin's 1947 Harley Davidson Knucklehead while courting Sue during the summers of 1964–1965. Bob remembered that they came to the Goat Hill Scramble on a date and found parking was arranged at the top of the hill and way above the house. The race track itself took advantage of the rest of the hillside, with a route circling around the house and stretching down the hill close to the highway.

Evidence of the Goat Hill races can be found in newspaper articles which reported, "A motorcycle race was held on Goat Hill on Sunday, June 21st, 1964, with a good-sized crowd" ["North on 71," *Sioux Rapids Bulletin Press*,

25 June, 1964, p. 8]. Then a second race was held on Sunday afternoon, July 26, 1964, when "a very large crowd attended the motorcycle races held at Goat Hill, six miles north of Sioux Rapids" ["North on 71," Sioux Rapids Bulletin Press, 30 July, 1964, p. 5.

GHOST CHASERS CLUB ACTIVITIES REMEMBERED

In an interview with Ghost Chasers club member Paul Currans, he jotted down a list of the Ghost Chasers Motorcycle Club activities that he knew were held after 1960:

- Several Rocket Runs
- Many Hill Climbs
- Dirt Track races and Enduros
    - » There was a dirt track race at Goodale Farm west of Spencer
    - » There was a dirt track race at Goat Hill south of Spencer
- Poker Runs
- Gypsy Tours
- Many Sunday or weekend fun rides
- Black Hills trips

Paul explained that the hill climbs, races, enduros, and Gypsy Tours were advertised for one and all, but the Ghost Chasers held a lot of "club only" events as well. The club only events would be the poker runs, rocket runs, and weekend group rides.

The Poker Run was an activity where the group would ride out to designated stopping places or checkpoints, sometimes at a bar. Once there, they would draw a playing card from the barkeeper or store owner to make up their hand of poker. Participants could travel at their own pace, but usually there was a designated end time when the group returned to their meeting spot. There they would see who had the winning hand of poker.

Paul Currans recalled one of his favorite events where "the guys had a lot of fun." It was a Rocket Run, and would be a night ride. A message would be sent out to members that a Rocket Run was to be held and to come to a designated spot. The riders were instructed to watch the sky to the east at

9:00 p.m. (for instance). The person designated as the launcher would set up maybe 10–15 miles away from the meeting point. The launching pad was prepared using about a five-foot steel tube with holes drilled into it a couple feet from the top so the fuse could be lit. A post hole digger would be used to secure that tube—maybe three feet deep—into the ground. The rocket would be placed in the tube and lit at the designated time. The launcher would set off the first rocket and wait, then set off another, etc., until the first rider found where they were located. That was the goal: to find whoever shot off the rocket.

The club would usually have around 12–15 bikes participating. Can you imagine the country roads at night and all of these motorcycles taking off at the same time? Paul recounts that they would travel fast—maybe 70–80 miles per hour, roaring down the gravel roads trying to locate that rocket launch site.

Paul Currans recounted an evening rocket ride where he was designated as the launcher. This would have been in 1962 or '63. The club members were told the location would be Lost Island Lake. All of the motorcycle riders expected that he would be shooting the rocket from the road on one side of the lake or the other. Instead, Paul went out on the lake in his cousin's houseboat and climbed on the roof and shot the first rocket off. Then he motored the pontoon over to the other side of the lake and shot another rocket, and kept moving the boat around the lake shooting rockets. Club members on their bikes were going crazy roaring around the lake looking for him. Finally, he pulled the houseboat into a dock area where they could find him. He chuckled when telling the story and said, "Boy, did I ever get cussed for that. And that was the last time they let me be the club's launcher."

Greg White shared a memory of a fun activity with the Ghost Chasers group where they were supposed to ride out to a designated spot and find an item hidden at that location, which they would bring back to prove they had been there. He recalled a humorous story where he thought he had found the correct location. He said, "So there was a tree and it was where an old swimming beach had been." And thinking that this tree was surely the spot were something was hidden, he said, "I reached in and pulled out a woman's Kotex from the crotch of that tree!" The Ghost Chasers group got a huge laugh out of that story, and Greg experienced some good-natured teasing that day. He said, "That wasn't too cool! That was not what I was supposed to find!"

Greg White also remembered a time he went with Marvin Jans to enduro races east of Sioux Falls. The Sioux Falls club was in a clubhouse right off highway 16 east of Sioux Falls. Greg recounted, "That was a pretty rough area out in there, and I was only 16, and Marv—that was Jeff's dad—he was probably 21. And I thought that was a big deal going out with the big kids, you know, to race my enduro. Well, I didn't do very well, of course. But the one thing I can remember is out in this rough old area there was an approach to what used to be a bridge across one of the rivers there… and the approach was there and the end of the approach was about 10 feet down to the land, and there was no bridge, and there was no warning at all, and I remember shooting up that and jamming on the brake and turning around and that's a true story." He said that it had been a fun time, but the scare of nearly launching himself and ending up at the bottom of that ravine was one that he often remembered, and it probably served to make him a more careful rider.

Weekend rides as a group were common. Paul Currans said, "On Sunday afternoons we would get together, ride together. By the end of the day, somebody's lights would be out and he'd be at the back riding home so ones with lights led the way."

Sheila Currans remembered, "One time when we were out riding with the group, some kids had put nails on the road. Several of us got flat tires. This was on the highway here local. We found out who had done it and the fathers of those boys felt terrible about it and came down and helped us change tires that day."

Paul Currans continued, "In the '60s we went to the Sturgis Rally… in a group, we hauled the bikes. I had a Triumph that I rode then. We took old Highway 14, 16… there was no interstate. Also, another route went through

Nebraska. There were no gas stations. We would fill up in Sturgis once we got across South Dakota. We usually camped in forest service camps. I remember one, Hanna Campground. We always would leave at midnight. It was so hot. We didn't have any air conditioning then. One time when we were traveling, we were making breakfast around 6:00 a.m., and Jerry Capesius's wife Carolyn accidentally dropped an egg and it fried right there on the road. Now that's South Dakota hot.

"The guys who rode spent time fixing their Harleys along the way—tighten chains, add oil. Where the Harleys parked there was always a puddle from the oil. I had a broken throttle cable once. Different things would need fixed. We always carried a tool kit with us. Mine had a hand pump, spark plug wrench, pliers, metric wrench."

Sheila Currans remembered trips to the Black Hills. "We rode on the back roads or trails in the Black Hills. There were numbered forest service roads… you were allowed to go through gates. One time we were out in the hills… on a Triumph… we went up a gravel road that was curvy. We slid on an incline and went down. A tire went flat. We were able to use the tire pump we carried and went on our way.

"One time we were up in the hills at our camp. The rest of the crew had gone to Spearfish to get supplies in the cars. There were lots of bikes left around the campsite. A family came driving in… saw the bikes… a lady came over to me and asked if it was safe to camp there. I told her it was safe, that I was one of the group with all the bikes. The lady turned out to be Maureen Horsely. She had grown up near the farm where Paul grew up!

"We had five kids and every time we went to the Black Hills some would come along. When we drove, the kids held up signs to show other cars on the highway. They thought that was a fun game. We also went to an enduro ride in Colorado one time. It was at the Rampart Range close to Denver."

I felt very fortunate to be able to spend some time listening to Paul and Sheila Currans reminisce about the good times they had as members of the Ghost Chasers. When I visited them at their home in the fall of 2024, I could tell immediately they both had a fair measure of Midwest humor and neighborhood spirit. Paul had parked his red 1950s-era Farmall H tractor in their front yard, decorated for Halloween with a full-size skeleton in the seat. He was looking forward to decorating it for Christmas as well, when the tractor would be draped in colored lights with a Santa Claus as the driver. They shared a wealth of information about the Ghost Chasers Motorcycle Club, and several pieces of documentation that got me on the trail to much of the research about the club. I was not to meet Paul again, as he passed away in the spring of 2025.

WINTER ICE RACING

Northwest Iowa motorcycle racers are year-round outdoorsmen. The average temperature in January is 26 degrees, with the average low being 7 degrees. It came as no surprise that the Ghost Chasers Motorcycle Club would be involved in winter motorcycle racing on area lakes. Jeff Jans, son of Ghost Chasers member Marv Jans, explained, "Sand was layered out on the ice for traction and racers added a third wheel to their bikes." Evidence of this was found in the *Spirit Lake Beacon*, dated January 17, 1963. The article confirms that the Ghost Chasers did indeed sponsor a motorcycle race at 2:00 p.m. Sunday, January 20, on Pleasant Lake, 3 miles east and a half mile south of Spirit Lake. The public was invited to come and watch at no charge ["Motorcycle Races," 17 January, 1963, p. 1]. There were several other winter ice races around the lakes that club members remembered attending.

Ice Racing on 5 Island Lake in Emmetsburg. Note side hacks on cycles.
(Photo courtesy of Tator Gilmore, Dean Gilmore collection)

Ice Racing on local lake, BSA cycle on left
(Photo courtesy of Tator Gilmore, Dean Gilmore collection)

CHESTELSON OPENS CORNELL CYCLE SHOP

Cornell, Iowa is located three and a half miles north of Sioux Rapids in Herdland Township. The post office there opened in 1901, but closed in 1967. Records show that in 1940, the population of the town was 21 citizens, and that number no doubt increased in the 1950s, only to begin to die out after that.

Today Cornell is an unincorporated farming community. Traveling the gravel road leading into the town today, one can see just a few inhabited houses, remnants of foundations, and old farm buildings. The Cornell school still stands, a classic two-story brick building built in 1914 for grades 1–8 but closed in the mid-1950s and later used as a town museum. The museum itself was organized and run by none other than Elmer Chestelson, who opened the Cornell Cycle Shop.

When I visited the site of the Cornell Motor Cycle Ranch in the spring of 2025, I found the building still standing. It has the appearance of a one-time feed store, and was probably built long before Elmer Chestelson opened it as a motorcycle business. The building was much smaller than I imagined, a paint-peeled wooden structure with a neglected ghost town appearance. There was a boarded-up side door on the west side which, I was told, was no doubt the mechanic's entrance. I could still see on the front of the building there was a wide garage-sized door which could have been lifted during business hours.

Originally, the shop also had a main entrance door located about in the center of the building, now boarded up. In a picture of the shop taken during its heyday, that entrance door is surrounded on each side by windows, each with six glass squares in a vertical row. On the right-hand side of the building, in the front, were four more vertical windows, approximately 1' by 6'. These are now gone. Bob Bendlin remembers riding out to this shop in

Cornell in the early 1960s to purchase special oil for the 1947 Knucklehead. He remembered that there was a wooden floor in the shop.

Ghost Chasers Motorcycle Club member Elmer Chestelson opened his motorcycle and scooter shop in Cornell in May 1961. The original name of the business was Cornell Motor Cycle Sales and Service ["Chestelson Opens Cornell Cycle Shop," 11 May, 1961, p. 1]. From an advertisement in the *Sioux Rapids Bulletin Press* dated May 18, 1961, the shop advertises that it has a showroom full of NSU motorcycles, motorbikes, and scooters. (NSU motorcycles were German manufactured, with the company founded in 1873 and acquired by Volkswagen in 1969.) In November 1961, another article in the *Sioux Rapids Bulletin Press* states that Chestelson has established a motorcycle shop and track at Cornell. In this article, the business name is now Cornell Motorcycle Ranch. He has added new model Harley Davidson motorcycles on display ["Chestelson Starts Motorcycle Ranch," 30 November, 1961, p. 1]. There is also an ad stating that Chestelson is an authorized dealer of Harley Davidson Motorcycles for Buena Vista and Clay County. The shop is open evenings and Sundays, offering a complete line of accessories, oils, parts, and repairs [Advertisement: "Cornell Motorcycle Ranch," 30 November 1961, p.6].

The shop continued business in 1964 when an article ran in the *Sioux Rapids Bulletin Press* about Mr. and Mrs. Elmer Chestelson attending a two-day show at the Harley Davidson Motorcycle National Dealership at Milwaukee. He announced that more information about the 1965 models was going to be available very soon at his shop in Cornell ["Chestelson's at Motorcycle Show," 23 July, 1964, p.1].

In November, 1967, there is mention of the shop again in the Sioux Rapids Bulletin Press, and the public is informed that the Motor Cycle Ranch in Cornell offers sales and service of motorcycles. It states that on Saturday afternoons and Sundays, a group of teens gather there to enjoy this fine sport of riding motorcycles, but adults will find plenty available for them as well ["Local Happenings," 3 November, 1967, p.6]. This shop is just a mile from Kindlespire Park, a popular destination for members of the Ghost Chasers

Motorcycle Club. No doubt it was a convenient place for a stop-off when riding a motorcycle through the area.

No record is found of the closure of the business. It seems that it simply faded away.

The Motor Cycle Ranch in Cornell in the 1960s

The Motor Cycle Ranch today

A COUNTY PARK IN CORNELL

Charlie "Chopper" Gilmore (Ghost Chaser member 1960s) shared that the Ghost Chasers Motorcycle Club members were instrumental in creating a county park in Cornell. The group worked hard to clear this park, creating trails and a picnic area. Located in southern Clay County, one mile east of the town of Cornell, Kindlespire Park is still used today and has grown to be a 310-acre wildlife area along the Little Sioux River. Today this public park complex includes the Burr Wildlife Area and Burr Oak Cemetery, as well as the Nelson Reng Wildlife Area.

Early Ghost Chasers club member Elmer Chestleton served as caretaker of this park for many years and was given an allocation of funds for improvement of the park seven years after the Clay County Conservation Commission took over management in 1965 ["Takes Little Used Park as a Project," *Sioux Rapids Bulletin Press*, 24 August, 1972, p. 1]. Elmer Chestleton owned the nearby Motor Cycle Ranch in Cornell, and he and his wife lived in Cornell and raised their family there as well.

While visiting this park, I could well imagine that it was a perfect picnic destination for the Ghost Chasers Club members on any weekend afternoon. A short ride of only about 30 minutes from Spencer, but off the beaten path, bordered on the east by the Little Sioux River, the park has numerous trails and picnic areas cut through. In the early years when the Ghost Chasers worked to clear the property, motorcycles were no doubt allowed to go on all of these trails.

THE GILMORE FAMILY

The breathtaking beauty of Clay County Iowa's rolling countryside and rich river bottomlands in the springtime is beyond compare. In May 2025, after thunderstorms had soaked the ground for several days with much needed rain, the land was glistening green, with so many shades of leaf and grass and richness that one's eyes felt rested in looking at it. I traveled south from Spencer on Highway 71 toward Sioux Rapids to visit with Charlie "Chopper" Gilmore about the Ghost Chasers Motorcycle Club.

Charlie "Chopper" told me of the early hill climbs sponsored by the Ghost Chasers Motorcycle Club that he first attended as a teenager when his enthusiasm for Harley Davidson motorcycles was ignited. At these hill climbs he eagerly volunteered to be one of the "catchers" on the hill, standing to the side and running out to grab onto the handlebars or any other catch-hold to prevent the out-of-control bikes from tumbling backwards down the hill and into the crowds of onlookers. He and his two brothers, Dick "Slider" Gilmore (Sturgis Hall of Fame) and Gary "Tator" Gilmore (twin-engine drag racing champion) cut their teeth riding their first Harley Davidsons on the country roads of Clay County, Iowa. It was Charlie and his uncle Dean Gilmore who became members of the Ghost Chasers Motorcycle Club in the 1960s.

The home where Charlie and his wife Toni live has been in the Gilmore family for five generations. The purpose of the visit was to have Charlie show me exactly where the Sioux Rapids Hill Climbs had been held, with a plan of touring his shop and then driving out to the hills by way of Cornell and Kindlespire Park. His knowledge of the area spans decades, indeed generations, as he told of the history of the various points of interest. As we talked, I came to know what most local people could have told me but didn't—I had just fallen deep into the presence of motorcycle stardom. All three brothers have lived their entire lives atop Harley Davidson motorcycles, each one making a name for himself in the world of biking.

In 1891, his great-grandfather, the first Charles Gilmore (b. 1852), arrived in Clay County from Clinton County, Iowa, and located on what was to become the family farm near Cornell. In 1895 Charles was elected to the Board of Supervisors of Clay County, where he served until 1912. In 1914, Charles was elected to the House of Representatives from Clay County and served in the 36, 37, 38, and 39th General Assembly.

He was instrumental in working with other Spencer area leaders to establish the very first Clay County Fair, held September 24, 1918. Billed as the largest agricultural exposition in North America, the fair continues to be one of the very largest county fairs in the country, now hosting over 300,000 visitors a year every September. Charles and his wife Clara A. Dickey raised their three children in that Sioux Rapids area farmhouse. His mother Charlott (b. 1830) also resided with them.

Their oldest child and only son, John Dickey Gilmore (b. 1892), followed in his father's footsteps, raising his own family in the house in which he grew up, farming the surrounding land. He married Pearl Sylvester and they had five children. Their oldest son Arlo became the third Gilmore generation to farm this land and live in the sprawling farmhouse. He and his wife Eleanor Julia Olson raised their six children nearby.

Arlo's younger brother Dean Gilmore (b. 1919) would forego farming and build his own successful engineering company in Spencer. His factory, Gilmore Engineering and Manufacturing (GEM) invented and produced the first fiberglass vaulting pole to be used in the Olympics. Dean Gilmore also invented and produced the first fiberglass fishing rods.

He also had a Triumph and Bridgestone dealership, selling these motorcycles from his shop in Spencer. In addition to riding motorcycles with the Ghost Chasers Motorcycle Club, often with his wife Irene alongside—his interests included flying. Dean was restoring an antique Jenny Airplane from 1915, remaking the wings and the engine. The iconic Curtiss Jenny biplane was produced in the United States from 1915–1919 as a World War I training aircraft. Dean planned on flying this two-seat open-cockpit plane with his nephew Charlie when it was completed. This was a project that was never finished, as Dean passed away in 1981.

The fifth generation to live at this farm was Arlo's son Charlie "Chopper" Gilmore. He was raised nearby, along with brothers Dick "Slider" Gilmore and Gary "Tator" Gilmore, and three other siblings. When the farm became available, Charlie and his wife Toni moved in and live there today, continuing the legacy of running a highly successful grain and livestock farm. At one time in the recent past, over 30,000 hogs were moved through the operation in a single year.

In the mix of growing up in the countryside along the Little Sioux River and graduating from high school, the Vietnam War happened, requiring that all men at age 18 register for the draft. This event would throw a serious monkey wrench into what had been an idyllic life in Midwest America. Charlie elected to enroll as an ROTC (Reserve Officer's Training Corps) student at South Dakota State University where he earned a degree in agriculture. This program allowed young men to make the required commitment to military service but would first provide them incentives to earn a college degree and then graduate as an officer in their chosen branch of the military. Upon graduation as a lieutenant, his enlisted life in the U.S. Army began.

Charlie spent one year at Fort Benning, Georgia, training in the infantry, and another year working in the legal department. His active duty continued in the jungles of Vietnam, where he served as a first lieutenant and combat platoon leader in the 101st Airborne Division, nicknamed the "Screaming Eagles." Aboard a Chinook helicopter flying into the war zone and back out again as quickly as it could, most often at night, Charlie and his platoon were dropped into combat areas and left deep in the jungles of Vietnam with orders to search and destroy. There they marched in the worst conditions imaginable, their bodies and boots constantly wet from walking through rivers and swampy ground. They lived off of C-rations which were periodically dropped to them.

At the end of three weeks, they would be picked up and taken to base camp, where they could receive medical treatment. The jungle rot on their skin could be treated and their feet could get a chance to heal. At the base camp, they did not get time off, but instead were assigned to routine jobs. This short reprieve from the highly dangerous and anxiety-producing stress of their mission allowed them time to regroup before the platoon was sent back into the jungle for a repeat search-and-destroy mission. Very shortly after Charlie's tour was up and he flew back to the United States, he received word that his entire platoon had been wiped out when their chopper went down on a mission gone wrong.

What does one do with an experience like that? Charlie Gilmore found his way by returning to a life of freedom on the back of Harley Davidson motorcycles, a long succession of them, rebuilding them, giving minute focus to the details of every nut and bolt and pipe and handlebar. While stationed in Fort Benning, Georgia, he had worked part time at a Harley Davidson garage repairing and rebuilding motorcycles. In the years that followed after he returned to Iowa, he has restored many kinds of motorcycles. Many are on display in museums, including the Sturgis Museum, where his restorations have received the highest ratings ever awarded at 99% grade for their closeness to the original factory models.

In addition to restoring old motorcycles to their original, he is a skilled builder of them. He has built choppers showcased not only in the United States, but Germany and Sweden. For the choppers sent overseas, the motorcycle enthusiasts from those countries would have Charlie fly over with the bike he was going to loan for display.

Quiet and unassuming, Charlie "Chopper" Gilmore, riding countless miles across the highways of this great country, also found a closer relationship with God and became an ordained minister and national chaplain for the Sons of Silence, of which he and his brother "Slider" are founding members. As he showed me around his garage and pointed out the row upon row of pictures from various events and rallies and banners and awards hanging on the walls above the work benches, there was a section with a picture of

Jesus alongside dozens of pictures of his fellow bikers who have passed on and requested that he be the one to officiate their funerals.

Charlie "Chopper" Gilmore's awards include the prestigious John "Farmer" Egger Award from the Motorcycle Riders Foundation (MRF) in 2010, and the coveted National Coalition of Motorcyclists (NCOM) Silver Spoke Award in 2022. He is a founding member of ABATE of Iowa's District 8. ABATE (A Brotherhood Aimed Towards Education) has a primary goal of working to promote safe riding practices through rider education and public awareness programs while advocating for motorcycle rights.

He is the recipient of the highly regarded 2025 Freedom Fighter Hall of Fame Award, from the Sturgis Motorcycle Museum and Hall of Fame. This award, which Charlie says he feels especially honored to receive, is given to individuals who have made significant and lasting contributions to the motorcycle community through defending the freedom and rights of motorcyclists.

He continues to ride countless miles on his motorcycles every year, making trips all around the United States as well as riding his motorcycle to Alaska. In the recent past, Charlie's trips have included motorcycle tours through eighteen different countries in Europe. He always makes a yearly trip to the Sturgis Motorcycle Rally held every August, and he will be there this year to celebrate the rally's 85th anniversary.

Still today, he and his wife come home from their travels to live and work in Clay County, Iowa. Of all the long list of past Ghost Chasers Motorcycle Club members, Charlie "Chopper" Gilmore is the most famous member and one who has done the most for the preservation and restoration of motorcycles and advancement of the sport of motorcycle riding, while protecting the rights and safety of motorcyclists on the roadways today.

BY-LAWS OF THE GHOST CHASERS MOTORCYCLE CLUB

Written in 1964

1. Roberts Rules of Order shall govern the parliamentary proceedings of this Club, unless otherwise provided in these By-Laws. Meetings shall begin promptly at eight o'clock. The order of business shall be

   a. Roll call

   b. Reading Minutes previous meeting

   c. Report of officers

   d. Unfinished business

   e. New business

2. The Club dues and meeting nights shall be decided at the beginning of each year. If dues are not paid by first meeting in March no more cards will be sent.

3. The principal place of business shall be within a radius of fifty miles of Spencer, Iowa.

4. All bills must be checked and approved by the Club before they are paid. Bills should be presented and paid by second meeting after Club's even.

5. Applications for membership must be recommended by two members of the Club. Upon payment of one year's dues, initiation fee of five dollars, and being voted in, applicant will be placed on probation for one year. The applicant may attend four meetings within six months before deciding to join or not. At the end of one year probation, his conduct being satisfactory, he becomes a member when voted in and entitles to all privileges of the Club. If voted out his initiation fee will be refunded.

6. A member may be expelled for conduct unbecoming a member of the Club, but charges must first be made in writing and the accused member given a hearing before the Board of Directors. The Board shall take evidence and report its findings to the Club with the recommendation that the accused member be expelled or the accused member remain in the Club. The Club shall thereupon take a vote to decide whether or not the recommendation of the Board be adopted. It shall require two-thirds vote of the members present at a special meeting to vote recommendation of Board.

7. All new members of the Club shall be members of the AMA.

8. Wives automatically become members when husband joins. She can vote the same as men members and joining the AMA is optional unless in competition where it is necessary.

9. One club emblem given to members paying initiation fee. More may be bought at fifty cents each until they are gone.

10. Honorary membership in the Club shall be given to any child of a Club member under sixteen years of age and belonging to the AMA. At the age of sixteen there will be no initiation fee required of them, but yearly dues as the other members.

11. Children under ten years of age are not allowed at Club meetings.

12. No alcoholic beverages allowed during any Club meeting.

13. Club members may bring guests to Club parties. If an admission is charged, he will be required to pay it.

14. The members' motorcycles should be road worthy as required by the laws of Iowa.

15. These By-Laws may be changed at any time the Club feels it necessary.

The original record book presented by Greg White shows Ghost Chasers member attendance at meetings. It is found that some members came for a short time and others stayed for years. The roll call shows members who attended one or more meetings from 1970–1979.

Mike Brandenburg	V. E. "Gene" Napier
Gwenn Brandenburg	Dorothy Napier
Paul Currans	V. E. "Junior" Napier
Sheila Currans	Judy Napier
Frances Ellis	Bobby Napier
Betty Ellis	Duane Rasmussen
Jim Farquahar	Ray Riecke
Jacky Farquahar	Helen Reicke
Russell "Dub" Gilbaugh	Gary Scheller
Dean Gilmore	Jay Shellabargar
Art K. Hansen	Sue Shellabargar
H. Maxine Hansen	Bob Sierck
Dick Heilstedt	Delores Sierck
Jackie Heilstedt	Richard "Red" Sorensen
Marvin Jans	Sue Sorensen
Norma Jans	Dale Studer
Tom Joines	John Studer
Sheryl Joines	Lois Studer
Mike Markley	Gary Tate
Carmen Markley	Kathy Tate
Roger Miller	Duane Vanderford
Linda Miller	Fern Vanderford
Tim Minor	Judy Minor
George Mundis	Donna Mundis

END OF AN ERA: GHOST CHASERS CLUB DISBANDS

Paul Currans shared a typed document—probably intended as a newspaper submission. It was dated June 30, 1999. It read, "Tuesday night, June 29, an era ended. The Ghost Chasers Motorcycle Club held their last 'official' meeting, bringing to a close a group that has been in existence since 1947." (Research shows the club actually started in 1938.) "Thirteen members were in attendance at a dinner gathering at Cindy's Steakhouse in Spencer. The club had once numbered as many as 50–60 members.

"Activities have been many and varied over the years. But their most successful activity was hill climbing. On a steep 100+ foot hill in Graettinger, they sponsored hill climbs that attracted competitors from Iowa, Minnesota, and South Dakota—and maybe a few more states! The event grew into a weekend of activities, usually beginning with an evening rocket run, then a morning poker run and afternoon hill climb. These events were more for fun than profit, but some money was accumulated over the dozen or so years they were held.

"As the members got fewer, and as liability insurance costs became prohibitive, it became obvious that the events would need to be discontinued. Seed money needed to sponsor the next event sat idle, except for a yearly night out for dinner for members. Tuesday night was the last of these dinners. Since the club charter had expired, members voted to dissolve the treasury as well. Two groups will receive about $500.00 apiece: American Cancer Society and Parent Project for Muscular Dystrophy Research, Inc.

"Members in attendance included Marvin & Norma Jans, Paul & Sheila Currans, Greg & Pamela White, Richard & Sue Sorensen, all of Spencer; Gene & Dorothy Napier of Cornell & Deming; MN, Mike & Sandy Markley of Ruthven; and Bob Napier of Webb."

Greg White recalled this decision. There was paperwork to be filled out and filed each year, and the interest had waned so it was decided to disband.

And so ended a motorcycle club that had lasted for sixty-one years. Through the decades, its members had formed friendships, met spouses, married, and raised children. They had enjoyed the great outdoors, seeing sights all around Northwest Iowa and into Minnesota and the Dakotas on jaunts lasting from a few hours to several days. They had lived their lives following the laws of the highway. But above all, they had fun together—and that, in the end, is a good life.

ACKNOWLEDGMENTS

This book would not have happened without the encouragement and help from my brother, Bob Bendlin. As a lifetime resident of Clay County, he had connections with the people in and around Spencer, Iowa, which allowed me access and interviews with so many. In addition, he had stories from his own youth that were different from mine, and he knew more about the locations and the motorcycles than I did. His help was invaluable.

I am grateful for Braden Falline, executive director of the Clay County Heritage Center, who put the initial bug in my ear to write this book. He knew firsthand that stories are history and history gets lost if it is not recorded. He also advised that objects are just objects without the story that accompanies them.

I appreciate the help given by Roby Miller Johnson at the Spencer Public Library, who was an eager supporter of my research. After I left Spencer in the fall of 2024, she promised to continue searching for newspaper articles that were not accessible to me online, and emailed them to me directly.

Thank you to Jeff Jans, who was an early help in gathering the research for this book. He gave me the first contact information for members of the club, loaned his dad's motorcycle jacket for display, and directed my research to include events such as those at Goat Hill and Graettinger.

I am indebted to Greg and Pam White, members of the Ghost Chasers, who shared records from the club that were significant in locating names of club members, as well as documents, pictures, and club memorabilia. They shared personal stories about the club that were so important to writing this history.

Heartfelt thanks to Sheila and the late Paul Currans, who invited me to their home to share their own memories of club events as well as lists of members and early documents from the club. Their kindness and interest gave me motivation to keep writing it down.

Much appreciation is due Joyce Singelstad Freeman, who lent support through sharing pictures and records of her father, Ernie Singelstad.

Thank you to my sister-in-law, Paula Bendlin, who shared her collection of dad's attire from his time in the Ghost Chasers, and for her persistence in finding "the" picture of him on his first Harley.

One of my later contacts in the writing of this book came after meeting Charlie "Chopper" Gilmore. His knowledge on the subject of anything to do with motorcycles is without compare, and I wish to thank him for the wealth of information he shared, including showing me where local hill climbs were held and much local history. He also brought his brother, Tator Gilmore, into the project. Tator shared many valuable pictures of the club.

Arla Kintigh was instrumental in connecting me to a much-needed professional proofreader and graphic designer, Michael Campbell at MC Writing Services in Omaha. The book would not have crossed the finish line without him.

Finally, I wish to thank my husband, Robert, who has been my encourager, my go-to sounding board, and the one who has patiently heard my daily frustrations and gone without much company as I became immersed in this project. I offer him this thank you and a promise to not start another writing project anytime soon.

ABOUT THE AUTHOR

Susan Bendlin Morgan is a farm girl at heart, raised in Clay County, Iowa. Her great-great-grandfather was a German immigrant who arrived in Iowa in 1871, homesteading on the tall grass prairie three miles southeast of present-day Langdon. She grew up with three brothers on a farm near this original homestead. She credits these Midwest roots for providing her with a strong work ethic and down-to-earth nature. Though she always calls Iowa home, she has spent her married life raising two daughters in the foothills of the Siskiyou Mountains near Grants Pass, Oregon, while leading 4-H clubs, cheering sporting events, and providing homes for a plethora of dogs, cats, and horses.

Susan earned a B.A. degree in Elementary Education from Southern Oregon University, and began the first half of her career teaching 8th grade students. She then earned her M.A. degree in Family Counseling from Oregon State University. She then worked as a school counselor, mentor teacher, and program developer, focusing on raising achievement levels in high-poverty schools. During this time she not only taught, but wrote grants to fund school-wide stringed instrument instruction, art and theater programs, and after-school programs. In this capacity, she led her school to a National Title One Distinguished School Award.

After retirement from the classroom, Susan has spent her time enjoying her grandchildren and gardening, as well as research. With a strong interest in genealogy, Susan enjoys piecing together stories from the past.

172

APPENDIX 1:
ALPHABETICAL
MEMBERSHIP LIST

Adams, Forrest (Spencer) member lists 1955, 1957

Anderson, Doris—1969*

Anderson, Jerry 1969*

Anderson, Kirby (Greenville) member lists 1953

Anderson, Johnny—1957*

Barglof, Duane (Greenville) member lists 1950, 1951, 1953

Barglof, Vernard (Greenville) member lists 1950, 1951, 1953, 1954, 1955

Bendlin, Clarence (Spencer) joined mid-1940s, member lists 1950, 1951, 1953, 1954, 1955, 1956, 1957

Beving, Lyle (Spencer) member lists 1953, 1954

Boatman, Jack (Peterson) member lists 1950, 1951

Booth, Arnold "Bud"—joined 1939–1941

Booth, Bob (Spencer) joined mid-1940s, member lists 1950, 1951, 1953

Brandenburg, Gwenn—active 1970s

Brandenburg, Mike—active 1970s

Brugger, Bill (Truesdale) member lists 1954, 1955

Capesius, Jerry—1954?* active 1960s

Chapman, John—1950?*

Chestelson, Bernie—1938 charter member

Chestelson, Elmer (Cornell) joined 1939–1941

Cox, Red—1957?*

Crone, Boyce (Webb) joined mid-1940s

Currans, Paul (Spencer) active 1960s, 1970s–1999

Currans, Sheila (Spencer) active 1960s, 1970s–1999

DePue, Bill—active 1960s

DePue, Judy—active 1960s

Dohlburg, LeRoy (Laurens) 1950?*

Doyle, Leo (Ayrshire) member lists 1950, 1951

Easton, Ralph joined 1939–1941, 1957

Easton, Jon (Spencer) active 1960s

Eaton, Billy—active 1960s

Edge, Bob—1969*

Edge, Darlene—1969*

Eischen, Jerry (Spencer) active 1960s

Ellis, Francis (Emmetsburg) active 1960s, 1970s

Ellis, Betty—active 1960s, 1970s

Erickson, Swede joined mid-1940s

Farquahar, Jacky—active 1970s

Farquahar, Jim—active 1970s

Fink, Dale 1954?*

Fulton, Bob 1938 charter member

Giep, Johnny (Spencer) member list 1953

Gilbaugh, Russell "Dub"—active 1960s, 1970s

Gilmore, Charlie "Chuck"—active 1960s

Gilmore, Dean—active 1960s, 1970s

Gilmore, Irene—active 1960s

Goyette, Al—joined 1939–1941

Grace, Bob (Mallard) active 1960s

Graham, Dick (Ruthven) active 1960s

Griffin, Dave (Ruthven) active 1960s

Hansen, Art K. (Spencer) active 1960s, 1970s

Hansen, H. Maxine (Spencer) active 1960s, 1970s

Hanson, Bob (Spencer) member list 1953

Hansen, Christie Albin—joined mid 1940s

Hielstedt, Dick—active 1970s

Hielstedt, Jackie—active 1970s

Hubbling, John (Ayrshire)—dues paid in 1951

Huisman, Don (Sheldon) member lists 1950, 1951

Ihry, John (Royal) member lists 1950, 1951

Jans, Marvin (Fostoria) joined mid-1940s, member lists 1953, 1954, 1955, 1956, 1957 active 1960s, 1970s–1999

Jans, Norma (Fostoria) active 1960s, 1970s–1999

Johnson, Phillip (Rolfe) 1954?*

Joines, Sheryl—active 1970s

Joines, Tom—active 1970s

Kabrick, Dale—1938 charter member

Ketcham, Darrell—1938 charter member

Knudtsen, Gary (Linn Grove) member lists 1955, 1956, 1957

Koenig, Bill (Ayrshire) 1950?*

Kress, Wayne (Webb) joined mid 1940s, member lists 1950, 1951

Lever, Jerry (Mallard) member lists 1950, 1951

Lewis, Lowell (Sioux Rapids) dues paid in 1950

Mansfield, Kenneth (Sioux Rapids)-joined mid-1940s, dues paid 1950

Markley, Mike (Ruthven) active 1960s, 1970s–1999

Markley, Carmen (Ruthven) active 1960s, 1970s–1999

Miller, Darryl (Spencer) member lists 1950, 1951, 1953

Miller, Linda—1968*

Miller, Roger—1968*

Mills, Bert (Webb) joined mid-1940s

Mills, Jerry (Greenville) active 1960s

Minor, Judy—active 1970s

Minor, Tim—active 1970s

Mohr, Dale "Bob?" (Spencer) dues paid 1950

Mundis, George—1968*, 1972

Mundis, Donna—1968*, 1972

Napier, Bob (Webb) active 1960s

Napier, Dorothy—active 1960s, 1970s–1999

Napier, Judy—active 1960s, 1970s

Napier, Robert A. "Bobby"—active 1960s, 1970s–1999

Napier, V. E. "Gene" (Cornell) joined 1960s, 1970s–1999

Napier, V.E. "Junior"—active 1960s, 1970s

Nesshoefer, Albert (Mallard) member lists 1950, 1951, 1954, 1955, 1956, 1957, active 1960s, 1970*

Nesshoefer, Ann—active 1960s, 1970*

Nielson, Bob—member list 1954, then "ARMY"

Nielson, Dorothy—member list 1954 with AMA #

Nielson, Howard—joined mid-1940s, member lists 1954, 1955, 1956, 1957

Nielsen, Roy (Spencer) joined mid-1940s, member lists 1950, 1951, 1953, 1954, 1955, 1956, 1957

Nordblad, Oscar (Ruthven) dues paid 1950, member lists 1955, 1957

Overeen, Gene—family member reports his membership in club

Parks, Bud—joined mid-1940s

Parks, Jim (Spencer) dues paid 1950

Peterson, Donald (Wallingford) member lists 1950, 1951, 1955

Rasmussen, Duane—1968*, 1970

Rasmussen, Linda—1968*

Rhodes, Arthur (Spencer) joined mid-1940s, dues paid 1950

Ridenour, LaVerne (Mallard) dues paid 1950

Riecke, Helen—active 1960s, 1970s

Riecke, Ray—active 1960s, 1970s

Santage Lee—joined mid-1940s

Scheller, Gary—active 1970s

Shellabargar, Jay—active 1970s

Shellabargar, Sue—active 1970s

Sierck, Bob—active 1960s, 1970*

Sierck, Delores—active 1960s, 1970*

Sievers, Don (Storm Lake) 1955? *

Singelstad, Ernie (Spencer) joined mid-1940s, member lists 1950, 1951, 1953, 1954, 1955, 1956, 1957

Smith, Robert—1950? *

Sorensen, Richard "Red" (Spencer) active 1960s, 1970s–1999

Sorensen, Sue—active 1960s, 1970s–1999

Stolley, Bill—1938 charter member

Studer, Bob (Rolph) active 1960s

Studer, Dale—active 1970s

Studer, John (Graettinger) active 1960s, 1970s

Studer, Lois—active 1960s, 1970s

Sweet, Fred (Webb) dues paid 1950

Tate, Gary—active 1970s

Tate, Kathy—active 1970s

Thompson, Lee—possible mid-1940s**

Vanderford, Duane—active 1968, 1970s

Vanderford, Fern—active 1968, 1970s

VanRenner, Richard Jr. (Sheldon) dues paid 1950

Wade, Lowell (Spencer) joined mid-1940s, member lists 1950, 1951, 1953, 1957

Watson, Milo (Milford) member lists 1955, 1956 1957

Webster, Wendell (Peterson) member lists 1950, 1951

Weiland, George (Truesdale) member list 1954

White, Arnold (Mallard) dues paid 1950

White, Greg (Spencer) member list 1957, active 1960s–1999

White, Pamela (Spencer)—active 1970s–1999

White, L.A. Jr.—joined mid-1940s

White, Vernie (Mallard) member lists 1950, 1951

Wills, Jerry (Milford) member lists 1955, 1956, 1957

Wills, Richard (Mallard) member lists 1954, 1955, 1957

Wolbur Kenneth (Sheldon) member lists 1950, 1951

Wright, Bob (Everly) 1938 charter member, member lists 1950, 1951

Young, Jesse (Sioux Rapids) joined 1939–1941

Zinn, Max (Storm Lake) member lists 1954, 1955, 1956, 1957

*Name appears in ledger list, then crossed out.

**likely member, he was listed as a flagman at 1947 Clay County Fairgrounds national race and evidence was found he owned a motorcycle. (Spencer Daily Reporter, 6/27/1941)

APPENDIX 2:
TIMELINE OF EVENTS

1938: Ghost Chasers Motorcycle Club formed with six charter members: **Bob Wright, Bob Fulton, Derril Ketcham, Bernie Chestelson, Dale Kabrick, Bill Stolley**

1939: Club grows to 11 members. New member identified: **Bud Booth**.

Oct. 8, 1939: Club holds first hill climb 2 miles east of Spencer on Highway 18

July 14, 1940: Club holds second hill climb 2½ miles east of Spencer on Highway 18 at Guy Huginon farm: 1000 watch

October, 1940: Draft registration for World War II begins

June 8, 1941: Club holds TT Races at new Motorcycle Sporting Course located 2½ miles east of Spencer, Highway 18

July 20, 1941: Third hill climb 2½ miles east of Spencer on Highway 18. Members identified: **Ralph Easton, Jesse Young, Al Goyette, Elmer Chestelson**

August 14, 1941: Club performs headlining act: Thrill Day at Buena Vista County Fair in Alta. "Widely known motorcycle daredevils doing spine tingling stunts."

October 19, 1941: Ghost Chasers lead a five-block-long parade when townspeople welcome over 700 Eagles who hold district meeting in Spencer

December 7, 1941: Pearl Harbor is attacked and U.S. enters World War II

1942: Club activities shut down. Rationing begins.

Sept. 15, 1942: Ghost Chasers ride in Parade of Freedom held in Spencer. This patriotic parade was attended by 7000 citizens

Sept. 2, 1945: World War II ends. Ghost Chasers Motorcycle Club reconvenes over next several months with new members joining: **Clarence Bendlin, Bob Booth, Boyce Crone, Swede Erickson, Christie Hansen, Marvin Jans, Kenny Mansfield, Bert Mills, Howard Nielson, Ray Nielson, Bud Parks, Art Rhodes, Lee Santage, Ernie Singelstad, Lowell Wade, L.A. White, Jr.**

Oct. 1, 1945: Ernie Singelstad opens Spencer Cycle Shop with Harley Davidson Dealership. (He arrived in Spencer July 1, 1945)

Aug. 25, 1946: Club holds TT Races on "new dirt track" 2 miles east of Spencer on Highway 18. Jess Young and Kenny Mansfield money winners in race. 750 spectators

Sept. 29, 1946: Club holds first hill climb in Sioux Rapids. 1½ miles east of town at the Oak Logvillion

Jan. 1947: Ghost Chasers Motorcycle Club file Articles of Incorporation with state of Iowa

July 6, 1947: Club holds second hill climb in Sioux Rapids. Location described as near Oak Logvillion. 500 watch.

July 20, 1947: Ghost Chasers Club sponsors AMA National Half Mile Race at Clay County Fairgrounds where 3000 watch. Club now has 31 members

June 27, 1948: Ghost Chasers Club sponsors second National Three Mile Motorcycle Championship Race at Clay Co. Fairgrounds. *Race delayed until Monday due to rain.

July 25, 1948: Club holds third hill climb in Sioux Rapids. Location near Oak Logvillion, but "new and better hill" 2½ miles East of where Highway 10 turns west

May 30, 1949: Ghost Chasers Club sponsors third National Half-Mile Flat Track race at Clay Co. Fairgrounds with $12000 purse

July 10, 1949: Club holds fourth annual hill climb in Sioux Rapids. Location same as year before near Oak Logvillion

May 7, 1950: Club holds fifth annual hill climb in Sioux Rapids. Location same as year before near Oak Logvillion

May 30, 1950: Ghost Chasers Club sponsors fourth annual National Motorcycle Classic AMA race at Clay Co. Fairgrounds. 5000 watch; 5 riders injured.

July 23, 1950: Club holds another hill climb (second this year) in Sioux Rapids. Location same as year before near Oak Logvillion

Sept. 3, 1950: Club holds another hill climb (third one this year) in Sioux Rapids. Location near Oak Logvillion. Benefit for Jess Young.

July 1, 1951: Club holds hill climb in Sioux Rapids. AMA-sanctioned. Location at the "Oak Logvillion hill" just east of town.

July 20, 1952: Club holds hill climb in Sioux Rapids at new location—"longer hill, more spills"—North of Sioux Rapids with signs erected from the bridge on Highway 71 to the site. Jess Young enters after broken back incident of 1950.

June, 1952: Okoboji Speed Bowl opens on Highway 71 just north of Milford.

June, 1953: Ghost Chasers Motorcycle Club sponsors motorcycle races preceding Stock Car and Midget Car Races at Okoboji Speed Bowl nearly every weekend during the summer season.

Aug. 1–2, 1953: Gypsy Tour held at Okoboji Speed Bowl. Early estimates expect 2000 motorcycles. Probably 800–1000 attend.

May 30, 1954: Okoboji Speed Bowl opens for season with AMA short track races sponsored by Ghost Chasers Motorcycle Club. Ernie Singelstad reported to be one of the six fastest riders.

July 4, 1954: Ghost Chasers sponsor motorcycle races which include TT races at Wallingford Ball Park

Aug. 6–7, 1955: Gypsy Tour held at Okoboji Speed Bowl. Over 1000 motorcycles attend.

1954–1955: Ghost Chasers member lists include **Clarence Bendlin, Roy Nielsen, Howard Nielsen, Ernie Singelstad, Marvin Jans, Albert Nesshoefer, Bill Bruger, Richard Wills, Max Zinn, Gary Knudtsen, Jerry Wills, Don Sievers, Milo Watson, Don Peterson, Forest Adams, Oscar Nordblad, Vernard Barglof, Jerry Capesius, Philip Johnson, Dorothy Nielsen**

July 4, 1956: Ghost Chasers sponsor motorcycle races, including TT races at Wallingford

1960s: Ghost Chasers Motorcycle Club continues with many old members as well as new. Member lists now include women: **Jerry Capesius, Paul and Sheila Currans, Bill and Judy DePue, Billy Eaton, John Easton, Ralph Easton, Jerry Eischen, Frances and Betty Ellis, Russell Gilbaugh, Charlie Gilmore, Dean and Irene Gilmore, Bob Grace, Dick Graham, Dave Griffen, Art and Maxine Hansen, Marv and Norma Jans, Mike and Sandy Markley, Jerry Mills, Gene and Dorothy Napier, Junior and Judy Napier, Bob Napier, Al and Ann Nesshoefer, Ray and Helen Riecke, Bob and Delores Sierck, Richard and Sue Sorensen, Bob Studer, John and Lois Studer, Greg and Pam White**

May 7, 1961: Ghost Chasers hold motorcycle races and field events in Graettinger, 2miles south on the River Rd.

May, 1961: Elmer Chestelson opens Motor Cycle Ranch in Cornell

July 2, 1961: Ghost Chasers hold hill climb in Graettinger, 2 miles south on the west side of the river

July 23, 1961: Ghost Chasers hold moto-cross scramble races in Graettinger

Aug. 30–31, 1961: Ghost Chasers hold camp-out, road run on Saturday, then field meet and hill climb on Sunday as part of Graettinger Labor Day Celebration. Event to be held at their "club grounds" south of town.

June 3, 1962: Ghost Chasers Motorcycle Club holds hill climb in Sioux Rapids. 1½ miles east of Sioux Rapids near the Oak Logvillion. *Postponed due to rain, held June 17 instead.

Sept. 2, 1962: Ghost Chasers hold hill climb event in Graettinger as part of Labor Day Celebration

Oct. 14, 1962: Ghost Chasers sponsor AMA motorcycle scramble race in Graettinger. One mile south of town, then east on the River Road

January 20, 1963: Ghost Chasers Motorcycle Club sponsors motorcycle races on Pleasant Lake, 3 miles east and a half mile south of Spirit Lake. Public invited, no charge.

Aug. 31, 1963: Ghost Chasers Motorcycle Club sponsors Scramble Races as part of 2-day Graettinger Labor Day Celebration, along with "Iowa Great Lakes Rally" to include camp-out, rocket run, field meet, and hill climb.

June 21, 1964: Motorcycle Scramble race held at Goat Hill

July 26, 1964: Motorcycle Scramble race held at Goat Hill

Sept. 6, 1964: Ghost Chasers host Hill Climb at Graettinger's 68th Annual Labor Day Celebration

1964: By-laws of Ghost Chasers Motorcycle Club written. *Probably the club had by-laws in place earlier and this was an update

1965, 1966: Ghost Chasers hold hill climb at Graettinger Labor Day Celebration

Sept 1–2, 1967: Ghost Chasers host rocket run on Saturday, followed by camp-out, then field meet and hill climb as part of Graettinger Labor Day Celebration

Sept. 1–2, 1968: Ghost Chasers hold rally and field events including a Powder Puff event as part of Graettinger's Labor Day Celebration

Aug. 30–31, 1969: Ghost Chasers hold road run and camp-out Saturday, field meet and hill climb Sunday as part of Graettinger's Annual Labor Day Celebration

1970–1971: Ghost Chasers continue to be part of Graettinger's Annual Labor Day Celebration, hosting hill climbs

1970–1979: Ghost Chasers member lists include the following: **Mike Brandenburg, Gwenn Brandenburg, Paul Currans, Sheila Currans, Frances Ellis, Betty Ellis, Jim Farquahar, Jacky Farquehar, Russell "Dub" Gilbaugh, Dean Gilmore, Art K. Hansen, H. Maxine Hansen, Dick Heilstedt, Jackie Heilstedt, Marvin Jans, Norma Jans, Tom Joines, Sheryl Joines, Mike Markley, Carmen Markley, Roger Miller, Linda Miller, Tim Minor, Judy Minor, George Mundis, Donna Mundis, V.E. "Gene" Napier, Dorothy Napier, V.E. "Junior" Napier, Judy Napier, Bobby Napier, Duane Rasmussen, Ray Riecke, Helen Riecke, Gary Scheller, Jay Shellabargar,**

Sue Shellabargar, Bob Sierck, Delores Sierck, Richard "Red" Sorensen, Sue Sorensen, Dale Studer, John Studer, Lois Studer, Gary Tate, Kathy Tate, Duane Vanderford, Greg and Pamela White, Fern Vanderford

1979–1999: Club activities change to become more "club only" recreational events which include Rocket Runs, Poker Runs, Weekend Fun Rides, club picnics, attendance at dirt track races, many day trips to the Lakes area, and longer trips to the Black Hills area for camping and Gypsy Tours

June 30, 1999: Ghost Chasers Motorcycle Club votes to disband, noting liability insurance costs and lower membership. *Another consideration is that Articles of Incorporation have expired after 50 years legal time limit. Members in attendance: **Marvin and Norma Jans, Paul and Sheila Currans, Greg and Pamela White, Richard and Sue Sorensen, Gene and Dorother Napier, Mike and Sandy Markley, and Bob Napier.**

REFERENCES

"The Gypsy Tours Are Coming," *Evening Times Republican*, 19 April, 1918, p. 7.

"Motorcycle Club Holds Outing at Lakes Area Sunday," May 26, 1937, *The Spencer Daily Reporter*, 26 May, 1937, p. 5.

"Motorcycle Rodeo," *The Spencer Daily Reporter*, 4 June, 1938, p. 8.

"Motorcycle Club to Be Formed Here," *The Spencer Times*, 26 January, 1939, p. 1.

"Spencer Motorcycle Club Invites Other Clubs to Meeting," *The Spencer Times*, 30 March, 1939, p. 1.

"Motorcycle Club Holds Meeting in Spencer," *The Spencer Times*, 13 April, 1939, p. 7.

"New 1940 Harley-Davidson Motorcycles," *The Spencer Times*, 7 September, 1939, p. 6.

"Wanted At Once! A HILL—!" *The Spencer Times*, 20 September, 1939, p. 5.

"In and Out of Spencer," *The Spencer Times, 5 October, 1939, p. 3.*

"Spencer Motorcycle Club Hill Climb Sunday," *The Spencer Times*, 5 October, 1939, p. 5.

"Motorcycle Hill Climb," ad in *The Spencer Times*, 5 October, 1939, p. 5.

"350 See Motorcycle Hill Climbing Events," *The Spencer Times*, 12 October, 1939, p. 5.

"In and Out of Spencer," *The Spencer Times*, 6 June, 1940, p. 3.

"Motorcycle Hill Climb," ad in *The Spencer Times*, 27 June, 1940, p. 7.

"Many Entries Listed; Motorcycle Hill Climb Is Set for Next Sunday," *The Spencer Times*, 4 July, 1940, p. 5.

"Cycle Event Set July 14," *Spencer Daily Reporter*, 10 July 1940, p. 1.

"Cycle Daredevils Will Compete Near Spencer," *Spencer Daily Reporter*, 11 July, 1940, p. 1.

"Motorcycle Hill Climb," ad in *Spencer Times*, 11 July, 1940, p. 12.

"Plans Completed for Motorcycle Events," *Spencer Daily Reporter*, 15 July, 1940, p. 1.

"1000 Watch Cycles Race Up Hillside," *Spencer Daily Reporter*, 16 July, 1940 p. 1.

"1000 Attend Motorcycle Hill Climb Sunday," *Spencer Times*, 18 July, 1940, p. 5.

"What Happened Here This Week," *Spencer Daily Reporter*, 22 July, 1940, p. 1.

"Local Men Escape Death in Accident," *Spencer Daily Reporter*, 9 September, 1940, p. 1, 8.

"Schedule Motorcycle Races at Alta Sunday," *Spencer Times*, 19 September, 1940, p. 5.

"Motorcycle Races," *The Graettinger Times*, 24 October, 1940, p. 1.

"Jesse Ditton Standing Beside His Farm Home," *The Sioux City Journal*, 17 November, 1940, p. 12.

"Ghost Chasers Are Hosts at Dinner Party," *Spencer Times*, 30 January, 1941, p. 4.

"Ghost Chasers to Stage 'Thrill' Day," *Spencer Daily Reporter*, 18 April, 1941, p. 6.

"Ghost Chasers Are to Start Season's Activities Sunday," *Spencer Times*, 24 April, 1941, p. 5.

"Ghost Chasers Hold Annual Spring Picnic," *Spencer Daily Reporter*, 28 April, 1941, p. 6.

"Motorcycle Races Sunday, June 8," ad in *Spencer Daily Reporter*, 6 June, 1941, p. 6.

"Many Watch Cycle Club Event Here," *Spencer Daily Reporter*, 9 June, 1941, p. 1.

"Buena Vista's Fair Planned." *Sioux City Journal*, 26 June, 1941, p. 5. Alta, Iowa.

"Large Number of Entries for Motor Cycle Climb," *Spencer Times*, 17 July, 1941, p. 5.

"Hill Climb is Set Sunday," *Spencer Daily Reporter*, 17 July, 1941, p. 5.

"Motorcycle Hill Climb," *Spencer Daily Reporter*, 18 July, 1941, p. 6.

"Record Is Shattered In Hill Climb Meet," *Spencer Daily Reporter*, 23 July, 1941, p. 6.

"New Hill Climb Record Set at Motor Cycle Event," *Spencer Times*, 24 July, 1941, p. 8.

"55th Annual Buena Vista County Fair," *The Sioux Rapids Press*, 31 July, 1941, p. 3.

"Fine Program Arranged for County Fair," *The Sioux Rapids Press*, 31 July, 1941, p. 8.

"County Fair Next Week," *The Sioux Rapids Press*, 7 August, 1941, p. 4.

McGrane, Bert in the *Des Moines Register*, reprinted in "Spencerian Sidelights," *Spencer Times*, 7 August, 1941, p. 2.

"Ghost Chasers Sponsor Thrill Day," *Spencer Daily Reporter*, 16 August, 1941, p. 6.

"White Injured When Motorcycle Crashes," *Spencer Daily Reporter*, 4 October, 1941, p. 1.

"Sick and Injured," *Spencer Times*, 9 October, 1941, p. 5.

"Eagles Hold Big District Meeting Here," *Spencer Daily Reporter*, 20 October, 1941, p. 1.

"Velma Borst and D. Ketcham Married Sunday," *Spencer Daily Reporter*, 3 November, 1941, p. 4.

Beck, B. "B-B Shots," *Spencer Times*, 6 November, 1941, p. 9.

"Two Big 3-Day Events Start in City Tuesday," *Spencer Daily Reporter*, 14 September, 1941, p. 1, p. 6.

"Annual Carnival Dance," *Spencer Daily Reporter*, 10 December, 1941, p. 5.

"Line of March for Parade is Listed Today," *Spencer Daily Reporter*, 15 September, 1942, p. 1.

"7000 Watch Parade Here Tuesday Night," *Spencer Daily Reporter*, 16 September 1942, p. 1.

"News of East Milford Vicinity," *The Milford Mail*, 16 November, 1944, p. 3.

****1945: No Articles Found in Newspapers about Ghost Chasers. This is the time they disbanded due to World War II and members drafted or enlisted.

"Kenny Mansfield in Motorcycle Spill," *Sioux Rapids Bulletin Press*, 13 June, 1946, p. 1.

"Cyclists hold *Gypsy Tour* after Midnight." *The Argus Leader*, 16 June, 1946, p. 14.

"Kenny Mansfield in Motorcycle Spill," *Sioux Rapids Bulletin Press*, 13 June, 1946, p. 1.

"Alta Scene of Motorcycle Races Sunday," *Sioux Rapids Bulletin Press*, 11 July, 1946, p. 1.

"Gypsy Tour to Cover Hills." *Rapid City Journal*, 1 August, 1946, p. 12.

"Gypsy Tour in Hills Friday." *Rapid City Journal*, 8 August, 1946, p. 4.

"Motorcycle TT Races," *Sioux Rapids Bulletin Press*, 22 August, 1946, p. 3.

"Local Boys Money Winners in TT Motorcycle Races at Spencer," *Sioux Rapids Bulletin Press*, 29 August, 1946, p. 1.

"Ghost Chasers Motorcycle Club to Hold Hill Climb in Sioux Rapids September 29," *Sioux Rapids Bulletin Press*, 26 September, 1946, p. 1.

"Fans Thrilled by Hill Climb," *Sioux Rapids Bulletin Press*, 10 October, 1946, p. 2.

Woodson, P. "Sporting Spotlight." *Rapid City Journal*, 4 January, 1947, p. 8.

"Cycle Club had Contest Here Sunday." *Kossuth County Advance*, 20 May, 1947, p. 3.

Morrell, W. "Thru the Hills." *Rapid City Journal*, 23 June, 1947, p. 7.

Woodson, W. "Sporting Spotlight," *Rapid City Journal*, 23 June, 1947, p. 6.

"Ralph Easton and His Orchestra," *Sioux Rapids Bulletin Press*, 3 July, 1947, p. 3.

"36 Hours of Turmoil—Stunting Motorcycles Run Riot in Streets," *Calgary Herald*, 7 July, 1947, p. 3.

"50 Injured in Motorcycle Riot in California Town," *Winona Daily News*, 7 July, 1947, p. 1.

"Hollister Recovers from Motorcycle Convention," *Martinez News-Gazette*, 7 July, 1947, p. 8.

"Streets of California Town Scene of Bedlam," *Corpus Christi Times*, 7 July, 1947, p. 7.

"Hill Climb Held in Sioux Rapids Sunday," *Sioux Rapids Bulletin Press*, 10 July, 1947, p. 1.

"Spencer Cycle Races Thrill 3,000 Fans at Fairgrounds," *Spencer Daily Reporter*, 22 July, 1947, p. 6.

"Cycle Races Sunday—Spencer, Iowa," *Sioux City Journal*, 18 July, 1947, p. 16.

"Ken Mansfield Injured in Motorcycle Accident," *Sioux Rapids Bulletin Press*, 7 August, 1947, p. 1.

"Scooptown Preparing for Tour and Races. "*Rapid City Journal*," 7 August, 1947, p. 14.

"Ken Mansfield in St. Joseph Hospital," *Sioux Rapids Bulletin Press*, 14 August, 1947, p. 1.

"Rider Hurt in Sturgis Cycle Tour," *Rapid City Journal*, 9 August, 1947, p. 1.

"Local News Items," *Sioux Rapids Bulletin Press*, 18 September, 1947, p. 1.

"Spencer Planning Three New Athletic Enterprises." *Sioux City Journal*, 4 April, 1948, p. 34.

"Ghost Chasers Make Plans for National Race," *Sioux Rapids Bulletin Press*, 8 April, 1948, p. 1.

"Set Motorcycle Races at Spencer June 27," *Sioux City Journal*, 21 April, 1948, p. 18.

"See Thrills and Spills at the National 3 Mile Motorcycle Race," *Sioux Rapids Bulletin Press*, 24 June, 1948, P. 7.

"Races This Afternoon," *Spencer Daily Reporter*, 28 June, 1948, p. 5.

Mackey, B. "Anthony Tops Riders," *Spencer Daily Reporter*, 29 June, 1948, p. 7.

"Motorcycle Hill Climb Here Sunday," *Sioux Rapids Bulletin Press*, 22 July, 1948, p. 1.

"Motorcycle Hill Climb Sunday," Ad in *Sioux Rapids Bulletin Press*, 22 July, 1948, p. 4.

"Black Hills Gypsy Tour," *Rapid City Journal*, 12 August, 1948, p. 1.

"Jess Young Takes First in Cycle Hill Climb Sunday," *Sioux Rapids Bulletin Press*, 12 August, 1948, p. 1.

"Jess Young To Race at Spencer Monday," *Sioux Rapids Bulletin Press*, 26 May, 1949, p. 1.

"Half-Mile Flat Track Motorcycle Races at Clay County Fair," *Sioux Rapids Bulletin Press*, 28 May, 1949, p. 4.

"Cycle Event Here Sunday, July 10," *Sioux Rapids Bulletin Press*, 7 July, 1949, p. 1.

"Motorcycle Hill Climb at Sioux Rapids," *Sioux Rapids Bulletin Press*, 7 July, 1949, p. 5.

"Young Second In Hill Climb Here," *Sioux Rapids Bulletin Press*, 14 July, 1949, p. 1.

"Fair Aug. 17–21 Alta, IA," *Sioux Rapids Bulletin Press*, 11 August, 1949, p. 6.

"500 Motorcyclists Compete in 2-Day Black Hills Classic," *Rapid City Journal*, 13 August, 1949, p. 1.

"Buena Vista County Fair August 17–21 in Alta, IA," *Rembrandt Booster*, Rembrandt, Iowa, 18 August, 1949, p. 2.

"Jess Young Takes Four Alta Races," *Sioux Rapids Bulletin Press*, 25 August, 1949, p. 1.

"Spencer Dotted with New Construction," *Spencer Times*, 8 September, 1949, p. 1.

"Two Hill Climbs Here This Season," *Sioux Rapids Bulletin Press*, 2 March, 1950, p. 1.

"Motorcycle Hill Climb Sunday," *Sioux Rapids Bulletin Press*, 4 May, 1950, p. 1.

"Large Crowd Views Motorcycle Event," *Sioux Rapids Bulletin Press*, 11 May, 1950, p. 1.

"Motorcycle Races Memorial Day," *Sioux Rapids Bulletin Press*, 25 May, 1950, p. 5.

"Five Injured in Motorcycle Races," *Spencer Daily Reporter*, 31 May, 1950, p. 2.

"Motorcycle Hill Climb Sunday," *Sioux Rapids Bulletin Press*, 20 July, 1959, p. 1.

"Motorcycle Hill Climb," Sioux Rapids Bulletin Press, 20 July, 1950, p. 5.

"Hill Climb Big Success Sunday," *Sioux Rapids Bulletin Press*, 27 July, 1950, p. 1.

"Benefit Hill Climb for Jess Young," *Sioux Rapids Bulletin Press*, 31 August, 1950, p. 1.

"A Benefit Motorcycle Hill Climb," *Sioux Rapids Bulletin Press*, 31 August, 1950, p. 5.

"Large Crowd at Benefit Hill Climb," *Sioux Rapids Bulletin Press*, 7 September, 1950, p. 1.

"Know Your Business Men," *Spencer Times*, 1 June, 1951, p. ?.

"Motorcycle Climb Sunday, July 1," *Sioux Rapids Bulletin Press*, 28 June, 1951, p. 1.

"Motorcycle Hill Climb Sunday, July 1," *Sioux Rapids Bulletin* Press, 28 June, 1951, p. 4.

"Return From a Motorcycle Trip," *Carroll Daily Times Herald*, Carroll, Iowa, 17 August, 1951, p. 6.

"Work on the Race Track Advances; To Open in May," *Spirit Lake Beacon*, 24 April, 1952, p. 1.

"First Races Sunday at New Okoboji Speed Bowl," *Milford Mail*, 5 June, 1952, p. 1.

"Opening Auto Races," *Milford Mail*, 5 June, 1952, p. 5.

"Stock Cars to Compete at Speed Bowl," *Milford Mail*, 12 June, 1952, p. 1.

"Stock Car Races at Okoboji Speed Bowl," *Lake Park News*, 12 June, 1952, p. 8.

"Motorcycle Hill Climb Sunday," *Sioux Rapids Bulletin Press*, 17 July, 1952, p. 1.

"Motorcycle Hill Climb Sunday," *Sioux Rapids Bulletin Press*, 17 July, 1952, p. 6.

"Jim Kearney Climbs Hill In 4.8 Time," *Spencer Daily Reporter*, 21 July, 1952, p. ?.

"Jess Young Wins Twice at Hill Climb," *Sioux Rapids Bulletin Press*, 24 July, 1952, p. 8.

"Motorcycle Races on Bowl Program," *Spirit Lake Beacon*, Spirit Lake, IA, 7 May, 1953, p. 8.

"Racing Scheduled for Two Days at Oko. Speed Bowl," *The Milford Mail*, 28 May, 1953, p. 1.

"Two Big Days of Racing," *The Milford Mail*, 28 May, 1953, p. 9.

"Want Ads," *The Cedar Rapids Gazette*, 29 July, 1953, p. 26.

"2000 Motorcyclists to Be in Territory Over This Week End," *The Milford Mail*, 30 July, 1953, p. 1.

"Motorcycle Parade to Tour Lakes Area," *Spirit Lake Beacon*, 30 July, 1953, p. 6.

"Testimony Taken at Dillon Murder Trial," *Sioux City Journal*, 28 October, 1953, p. 14.

"Okoboji Speed Bowl to Open Thursday, Jun 3," *Milford Mail*, 20 May, 1954 p. 1.

"Motorcycle Races," *The Milford Mail*, 27 May, 1954, p. 8.

"Motorcycle Stock Car Races at Speed Bowl Next Week," *The Milford Mail*, 27 May, 1954, p. 1.

"Four Wins Scored by Rider in Cycle Race," *Spencer Daily Reporter*, 1 June, 1954, pg. ?.

"Okoboji Speed Bowl Races to Open on Thursday," *Milford Mail*, 3 June, 1954, p. 1.

"List Full Day's Program for Wallingford's Third Annual Big July Fourth Celebration," *The Graettinger Times*, 1 July, 1954, p. 1.

"Cyclists to Hold Race at Arnolds Park," *Spencer Daily Reporter*, 1 August, 1955, p. ?.

"More Than 1,000 Motorcycles in Area Over Week End; Attend Gypsy Tour," *The Milford Mail*, 11 August, 1955, p. 1.

"Wallingford To Celebrate July Fourth," *The Graettinger Times*, 28 June, 1956, p. 1.

"Motor Maid Winner," *The Daily Times*, Davenport, Iowa, 6 August, 1957, p. 16.

"Jack Paul Killed in Plane Crash in Italy," *The Lake Park News*, 16 April, 1958, p. 1.

"Want Ads," *Cedar Rapids Gazette*, 2 August, 1958, p. 10.

"Motorcycle Field Trials Here Sunday," *The Graettinger Times*, 4 May, 1961, p. 1.

"Chestelson Opens Cornell Cycle Shop," *Sioux Rapids Bulletin Press*, 11 May, 1961, p. 1.

"Cornell Motorcycle Sales & Service," *Sioux Rapids Bulletin Press*, 18 May, 1961, p. 2.

"Cycle Hill Climb Sunday Afternoon," *Sioux Rapids Bulletin Press*, 14 June, 1961, p. 1.

"Motorcycle Hill Climb Here Sunday Afternoon," *The Graettinger Times*, 29 June, 1961, p. 1.

"Large Crowd at Cycle Hill Climb," *The Graettinger Times*, 6 July, 1961, p. 1.

"List Results of Recent Motorcycle Scramble Races Here," *The Graettinger Times*, 3 August, 1961, p. 6.

"Announce Labor Day Program for Two-Day Celebration," *The Graettinger Times*, 21 August, 1961, p. 1.

"Chestelson Starts Motorcycle Ranch," *Sioux Rapids Bulletin Press*, 30 November, 1961, p. 1.

"Cornell Motorcycle Ranch," *Sioux Rapids Bulletin Press*, 30 November, 1961, p. 6.

"Cycle Scramble Race Has Been Cancelled," *The Graettinger Times*, 21 June, 1961, p. 1.

"Classified Want Ads," *Sioux Rapids Bulletin Press*, 24 May, 1962, p. 8.

"Cycle Hill Climb Sunday Afternoon," *The Sioux Rapids Bulletin Press*, 14 June, 1962, p. 1.

"Plans Progressing for 66th Annual Labor Day Celebration," *The Graettinger Times*, 23 August, 1962, p. 1.

"Graettinger's 3-Day Labor Day Celebration," *The Graettinger Times*, 30 August, 1961, p. 7.

"66th Labor Day Celebration," *The Graettinger Times*, 30 August, 1961, p. 1.

"Celebration Well Attended; Coot and Rainy Labor Day," *The Graettinger Times*, 6 September, 1962, p. 1.

"Motorcycle Scramble Races Here Next Sunday Afternoon," *The Graettinger Times*, 11 October, 1962, p. 1.

"Motorcycle Races," *The Spirit Lake Beacon*, 17 January, 1963, p. 1.

"Motorcycle Scramble Races Slated Here on Memorial Day," *The Graettinger Times*, 23 May, 1963, p. 1.

"Motorcycle Scramble Races," *The Graettinger Times*, 23 May, 1963, p. 5.

"Motorcycle Scramble Races Slated Here on Memorial Day," *The Graettinger Times*, 30 May, 1963, p. 1.

"Motorcycle Scramble Races," *The Graettinger Times*, 30 May, 1963, p. 3.

"Graettinger's 3-Day Labor Day Celebration," *The Graettinger Times*, 29 August, 1963, p. 7.

"Motorcycle Rally Here This Weekend," *The Graettinger Times*, 29 August, 1963, p. 1.

"Cycle Hill Climb Draws Large Crowd and Many Entries," *The Graettinger Times*, 5 September, 1963, p. 1.

"North on 71," *Sioux Rapids Bulletin Press*, 25 June, 1964, p. 8.

"Chestelsons at Motorcycle Show," *Sioux Rapids Bulletin Press*, 23 July, 1964, p. 1.

"North on 71," *Sioux Rapids Bulletin Press*, 30 July, 1964, p. 5.

"68th Labor Day Celebration," *The Graettinger Times*, 3 September, 1964, p. 1.

"7.6 Inches of Rain Here Labor Day, Flooding Follows," *The Graettinger Times*, 10 September, 1964, p. 1.

"Many Events Being Planned for Labor Day," *The Graettinger Times*, 5 August, 1965, p. 1.

"69th Annual Labor Day Celebration," *The Graettinger Times*, 2 September, 1965, p. 1.

"Labor Day Celebration," *The Graettinger Times*, 2 September, 1965, p. 7.

"70th Annual Celebration Here This Year," *The Graettinger Times*, 28 July, 1966, p. 1.

"Annual Labor Day Program for 70th Annual Celebration," *The Graettinger Times*, 25 August, 1966, p. 1.

"70 Annual Labor Day Celebration," *The Graettinger Times*, 1 September, 1966, p. 1.

"Labor Day Celebration," *The Graettinger Times*, 1 September, 1966, p. 7.

Photos "Labor Day 1966," *The Graettinger Times*, 8 September, 1966, p. 1.

"List Results of Cycle Hill Climb," *The Graettinger Times*, 15 September, 1966, p. 1.

"Announce Labor Day Program For Friday, Saturday, Sept. 1,2," *The Graettinger Times*, 24 August, 1967, p. 1.

Advertisement, "Labor Day Celebration," *The Graettinger Times*, 31 August, 1967, p. 7.

"Motorcycle Hill Climb Results Are Listed," *The Graettinger Times*, 7 September, 1967, p. 1, p. 7.

"Local Happenings," *Sioux Rapids Bulletin Press*, 30 November 1967, p. 6.

Photos "More Labor Day Views," *The Graettinger Times*, 12 June, 1968, p. 1.

"Good Crowds Attend the Horse Show and Hill Climb," *The Graettinger Times*, 5 September, 1968, p. 1.

"Motorcycle Hill Climb Results, Sue Studer Places in Powder Puff Event," *The Graettinger Times*, 19 September, 1968, p. 6.

"Number of Events Already Planned for Labor Day," *The Graettinger Times*, 14 August, 1969, p. 1.

"Hill Climb August 30 & 31—Graettinger," *The Graettinger Times*, 28 August, 1969, p. 5.

"Attend Graettinger's 73rd Annual Labor Day Celebration," *The Graettinger Times*, 28 August, 1969, p. 6.

"Results of Hill Climb Events," *The Graettinger Times*, 4 September, 1969, p. 1.

"Announce Plans for 74th Annual Graettinger Labor Day Celebration," *The Graettinger Times*, 13 August, 1970, p. 1.

"74th Annual Labor Day Celebration Here!" *The Graettinger Times*, 3 September, 1970, p. 1.

"Attend Graettinger's 74th Annual Labor Day Celebration," *The Graettinger Times*, 3 September, 1970, p. 3.

"7.6 Inches of Rain Here Labor Day, Flooding Follows," *The Graettinger Times*, 2 September, 1971, p. 7.

"Labor Day Diamond Jubilee Celebration Big Success," *The Graettinger Times*, 9 September, 1971, p. 1.

"Cornell Museum Open May 14," *Sioux Rapids Bulletin Press*, 4 May, 1972, p. 1.

"Takes Little Used Park on as Project," *Sioux Rapids Bulletin Press*, 24 August 1972, p. 1.

Reiser, S. "The Roadrunners... Local residents find fellowship in motorcycles," *Spirit* Lake Beacon, 4 June, 1981, p. 4.

Mills, D. "Clay County Fair Promoted at Goat Hill," *Sioux Rapids Bulletin Press,* 27 August, 1981, p. 2.

Reiser, S. "Economy Run Planned," The Spirit Lake Beacon, 22 June, 1982, p. 3.

Wallace, L., "The Farmer's Wife," Lake Park News, 1 September, 1983, p. 5.

"Touring Singelstad Barns," *The Northwood Anchor,* 3 May, 2023, p. 6.

Made in the USA
Monee, IL
29 July 2025